"I wish this book was out when I first became a Christian! What we believe really matters, and this book covers many basic and necessary beliefs of the Christian faith in an easy-to-read format. It's like sitting in a theology class, but one that brings life and you can understand what the teacher is teaching. There has been no more urgent time in history for us to be reading and learning the basic beliefs of the Christian faith. I encourage all Christians, especially those new to the faith, to not miss the joy and wonder of learning what is written in this book."

Dan Kimball, Pastor, Vintage Faith Church; author,
They Like Jesus but Not the Church

"As a pastor I'm often confronted by new Christians with questions such as: "How do I get started? What should I read? How do I grow spiritually? Although I haven't had good answers in the past, I do now. I'm sending them to Michael Patton's excellent book. This is a gem! Eminently readable and experientially relevant, this is a book that addresses with brutal but always loving honesty the most pressing theological issues a new believer faces. In fact, you who are a bit older in the faith can also benefit from Michael's insights. Highly recommended for Christians of all ages!"

Sam Storms, Senior Pastor, Bridgeway Church,
Oklahoma City, Oklahoma

"If you want to grow in your faith as a new Christian, or if you just need to get back to the long-neglected basics, Michael Patton will prove to be a wise guide. *Now That I'm a Christian* is not only practical and easy to follow; it is biblically balanced and theologically informed. What a ready resource to help churches, campus ministries, and individual spiritual mentors to train new believers in the faith!"

Paul Copan, Pledger Family Chair of Philosophy and Ethics,
Palm Beach Atlantic University; author, *Loving Wisdom: Christian Philosophy of Religion*

"Rolled into this one volume is a guide to both right belief and right practice. Believers need a solid foundation that maps out the essentials for the Christian faith, as well as how to grow stronger and deeper in that faith. This work addresses both. Written in an introductory manner that is well-informed, witty, and fast-paced, readers will feel at home in the text even if they have not studied these things before. I recommend it with pleasure."

Gary R. Habermas, Distinguished Research Professor & Chair,
Philosophy Dept, Liberty University

Now That I'm a Christian

Now That I'm a Christian

WHAT IT MEANS TO FOLLOW JESUS

C. Michael Patton

WHEATON, ILLINOIS

Now That I'm a Christian: What It Means to Follow Jesus

Copyright © 2014 by C. Michael Patton

Published by Crossway
            1300 Crescent Street
            Wheaton, Illinois 60187

Cover design: Faceout Studio

First printing 2014

Printed in the United States of America

Unless otherwise indicated, Scripture quotations are from the ESV® Bible (*The Holy Bible, English Standard Version*®), copyright © 2001 by Crossway. 2011 Text Edition. Used by permission. All rights reserved.

Scripture quotations marked AT are the author's translation.

All emphases in Scripture quotations have been added by the author.

Trade paperback ISBN: 978-1-4335-3804-9
ePub ISBN: 978-1-4335-3807-0
PDF ISBN: 978-1-4335-3806-3
Mobipocket ISBN: 978-1-4335-3805-6

Library of Congress Cataloging-in-Publication Data
Patton, C. Michael, 1972–
   Now that I'm a Christian : what it means to follow Jesus
/ C. Michael Patton.
      pages cm
   Includes bibliographical references and index.
   ISBN 978-1-4335-3804-9
   1. Theology, Doctrinal—Popular works. 2. Christian
life. I. Title.
BT77.P345   2013
230—dc23   2013026735

Crossway is a publishing ministry of Good News Publishers.

VP		24	23	22	21	20	19	18	17	16	15	14
15	14	13	12	11	10	9	8	7	6	5	4	3	2	1

Contents

Introduction

I can't wait to tell you about your new faith. I can't wait to tell you about Jesus, the Bible, prayer, and all the wonderful things we are going to cover in this book. You are a disciple of Christ, and I intend to give you a solid start that will ground you in the most important issues that have defined Christianity for the last two thousand years. You are a Christian. Welcome to the family.

What does it mean to be a *disciple*? That term may be foreign to you. But don't worry. You don't have to grow a beard or put on a robe. You may have heard of the twelve disciples of Christ. Well, being a disciple of Christ—being a Christian—is like that. To be a disciple means being a student of someone. But it is much more than that. In the time of Christ, when people were disciples of someone else, they placed themselves completely under that person's authority in both education and lifestyle. Their goal was to become exactly like their mentor. This is how the disciples were with Christ. They left everything and followed him. They went everywhere he went, did everything he did, and believed everything he believed (at least, they tried!). And, over two thousand years later, we have this same privilege. We, too, become disciples of Christ the moment we trust in him. I can't wait to take your hand on this journey.

You might be thinking, *can a book make me a disciple of Jesus?*

It would be naive to believe such a thought. Discipleship cannot be carried to completion through a book. Is it a waste of my time, therefore, to write a book such as this? No. You *should* read this book. I think you will soon find out why.

Jesus commanded all who would follow him to take up their cross and follow him. Discipleship is not something you do on the side. It is not a part-time job. It affects and infects every part of your being, everything that you do, and everything that you are. It is really difficult to be a Christian without being a disciple. Why would you want to be? When you bow the knee to Christ, you declare him to be God and Lord of the universe. This does not mean that you are always a *good* disciple or that you do everything right. This does not mean that we don't fall on our face over and over. I certainly do. It means that we are on a path following the eternal God. And this path beckons us to pick ourselves up every time we fall.

Christ told his disciples to "go therefore and make disciples . . . teaching them to observe" everything he had commanded (Matt. 28:19–20). This command has become so famous, it is better known today as "The Great Commission." We will talk a lot about the Great Commission in the last chapter. But know this: Christ's command to follow him is more than a command; it is a wonderful privilege. It is a *great* privilege.

My aim is to point you in the right direction for a lifetime of following Christ. My prayer is for you to spend the rest of your life growing in your discipleship of Christ. When you attempt to do this on your own, however, Christ-following can be a dangerous and often confusing road. You can easily get sidetracked and lost. I will give you a basic road map that you can look back to time and time again to help find your way and reinvigorate your faith when it wanes.

NEED FOR DISCIPLESHIP

It's popular today to think that learning about God will stifle our passion for God. I've even heard people say, "I'd rather be led instead of read." While I understand what such people are concerned about, we need to be careful. Anyone passionate in any subject will seek to learn more and more about the subject. People who are passionate about wine become students of wine. They learn about the art of wine making, differing varieties in differing climates, soil nutrients, fermentation, barreling, pairing, and proper tasting techniques. They love the taste, but the taste is greatly enhanced by their knowledge. People who are passionate about NASCAR become students of NASCAR. They learn the history of certain racetracks, they will tell you about some of the great drivers from the past, and they'll gain knowledge about fuel conservation during a race, driver and fan safety, getting the most out of the tires, and driver g-forces. And don't get me started on football fans. You get the picture.

If you have trusted in Christ, your eternal destiny has been altered by a Savior who lived, died, and rose in your place. He invites you to trade your heavy burden in exchange for his light yoke. Your God is with you every day and is leading you safely to your eternal home. Yet so many people will go months, years, or even a lifetime without taking the initiative to grow as a learner.

LAYOUT OF THE BOOK

This book provides you with the foundations for discipleship. The first half of the book will focus on *orthodoxy*. The second half will cover *orthopraxy*.

For those who might suffer from terminology anxiety, *orthodoxy* simply means "straight teaching" or "worship." People go to the *ortho*dontist to get their teeth straightened. *Orthodoxy* is meant to straighten your doctrine! You can't act upon what you don't know. All of our obedience is based on a correct understanding of who God is and what he has done for us. Getting this foundation down will drive you, with great excitement, to the path of discipleship. You will say to yourself, "If Jesus has really done all of this for me, I can't wait to join him and become a colaborer for the truth he has revealed." It's like if you were to discover the cure for cancer. Wouldn't you tell everyone you know? The knowledge is foundational. But the response is what changes the world. You have discovered the cure for souls. You have discovered the love of God. It is much greater than the cure for cancer, and the disease that people are infected with, as we will see, is much more dangerous than cancer. Orthodoxy provides a foundation and a motivation for all that we do for God.

If you have been around churches, Christians, or religious conversations, the word *orthodoxy* might scare you. After all, which Christian orthodoxy are we talking about? Yours? Baptist's? Catholic's? Presbyterian's? Eastern Orthodox's? When I say *orthodoxy*, I am talking about "that which has been believed always, everywhere, and by all." This is called the Vincentian Canon, named for fifth-century writer St. Vincent of Lérins. It expresses the need for unity in doctrine. While there have indeed been many issues that Christians have disagreed about over the years, there are many more that have united us. For example, in chapter 3 we will talk about the need to believe in the Trinity, as expressed in this book. Christians of all times and of all places have agreed about the doctrine of the Trinity. It is an essential of orthodoxy. We will examine five such essential beliefs about which there is virtually no debate among

Protestants. However, when you get to the chapters on authority, man, and faith, you will see that there are a few issues that distinguish Protestants from Catholics and Eastern Orthodox. However, even with these topics, there is significant general agreement. For example, Protestants argue that justification is by faith alone (*sola fide*). Roman Catholics, on the other hand, do not believe that justification is by faith alone. Nevertheless, they would emphasize the absolute essentiality of faith and agree with my definition of what Christian faith is (more on this in chap. 5).

While *orthodoxy* refers to having correct thought or right beliefs, *orthopraxy* refers to right practice. In the second half of the book, we are going to discuss five practices that all Christians of all time have agreed about. From prayer to outreach, Christianity has been united in believing that these disciplines are essential for Christian discipleship.

Here are the topics that will be covered in each chapter:

Orthodoxy

- Bible
- Man
- God
- Christ
- Faith

Orthopraxy

- Prayer
- Study
- Church
- Suffering
- Mission

Lord, I pray that these next ten chapters will deepen your servants' love and knowledge of you. You beckon us to grow in you as we live this life in the world you've created. May we be teachable and delight in the process of learning more about you so we can live more passionately and accurately for you.

1

Bible

When I was a kid, I would manipulate my parents. I would ask my mom if I could go over to my friend Wayne's house, only to be told that it was too late at night or that the family had other plans. Upon receiving the answer I did not want from Mom, I would seek the authority of Dad. "Dad, can I go over to Wayne's house?" "Sure," would come the response. Now my desire was covered. I could go over to Wayne's house with a clear conscience. Though two major authorities (Mom and Dad) clashed in my life, I felt free to obey the one whose answer I liked best.

As you can imagine, that kind of result did not happen often. In fact, the manipulation eventually came to a screeching halt. Problem: Mom and Dad talked! After a while, my dad's answers to such questions became depressingly rote: "Go ask your mom," or "What does your mom say?" Dad would not play the game. He would always punt to Mom. The authority became united with no conflicts. In essence, with this type of stuff, Mom was the final and only infallible authority!

Your Christian life is not so different. When we first become Christians, the biggest question is, now what? What should I expect? Where should I go? Who do I ask? What should I believe? What do I do? Who do I trust? Who has the final say? We look for sources of authority to guide and direct our lives, and we have all kinds of options (Moms and Dads, if you will). And you know what? These options will not always agree. So where do you go for authority in your Christian walk?

THE BIBLE

The first authority in our lives is the Bible. In Protestant circles we use the fancy Latin phrase *sola Scriptura*. The doctrine of *sola Scriptura* means that the Bible is the final and only infallible source of authority for our faith. We might say the Bible is the "ultimate authority" or the "eternal trump card" (for those who like to play cards). We will talk more about *sola Scriptura* shortly, but hang with me as I tell you a bit about the Bible.

The Bible is a collection of sixty-six ancient books. I am not sure that "books" is the best way to put it, but it will do for now. The Bible is made up of history, poetry, personal letters, community letters, genealogies (that sometimes seem endless!), short pithy statements of good advice, eternal laws, temporal laws, and biography. The oldest books of the Bible date from around 1,500 years before Christ. The last book dates to the end of the first century. No books have been added to the Bible since its completion, and Christians don't expect to ever have anything else added to it.

The books that make up the Christian Bible are called the *canon* of Scripture. (*Scripture* and *Bible* are often used interchangeably. They mean the same thing.) Protestant Christians hold to a sixty-six book canon (Catholics add a few to the Old Testament, called the *Deuterocanonical* books or the *Apocrypha*).

The Bible is divided into two *testaments* or *covenants*. The first testament is called the Old Testament. It deals with the general history of man, his creation by God, his fall into sin, and God's promise to fix what man, through sin, broke (we will talk more about that in the next chapter). The primary focus of the Old Testament is the nation of Israel. God gave the nation of Israel a promise through the father of the nation, Abraham. God said that, in his old age, Abraham would have a son, and one of his descendants would become a great blessing to the whole world. We later come to know this great blessing as the *Messiah* or *Redeemer* (i.e., the one who will fix everything). Though the Israelites did not know exactly what to look for, they waited anxiously for this Messiah. The second testament is called the New Testament. While the Old Testament covers thousands of years, the New Testament puts on the brakes and covers about seventy-five to one hundred years. Its primary focus is on the Messiah promised in the Old Testament. This Messiah is Jesus Christ, the very Son of God. How did God fix everything? Through sending his Son, God in the flesh, to take the punishment for the sins of God's people on a wooden cross. The New Testament is an account of this sacrifice and the implications that it should have on our lives.

Deep breath.

While the Bible is a story about what we are to believe concerning God, the fall, and the salvation of man, it is also a kind of instruction book on how to live. By both direct command and example, it teaches us what God's will is for our lives. The Bible is called "God's Word." This means that when it speaks, God speaks. We call this *inspiration*. While God is very involved in all of history (as we will see) and we should expect his movements through experiences in our lives, we should *not* expect to actually hear his literal voice or see his literal face. He speaks to us through his Word, the Bible.

Notice what Paul says concerning the Bible:

> All Scripture is breathed out by God and profitable for teaching, for reproof, for correction, and for training in righteousness, that the man of God may be complete, equipped for every good work. (2 Tim. 3:16–17)

The Bible equips us for *every* good work, not just some good works. It is given to make you a competent disciple. The Greek word for *inspired* literally means "God breathed." Can you believe that? The Bible is the breath of God! Every word in the Scriptures is exactly what God wanted to write. However, God used over forty men from all walks of life—from fishermen to kings—to write his Word, and he did not sacrifice their personality or circumstances in the least. This is one of the great mysteries of Scripture.

Peter puts it this way: "For no prophecy was ever produced by the will of man, but men spoke from God as they were carried along by the Holy Spirit" (2 Pet. 1:21). In other words, as these men wrote the Scriptures, they were carried along by the Spirit as a boat is carried along by the wind. God used man by moving through their thoughts and words.

We will return to the authority of Scripture in a moment. But before we do, we need to look at four other sources that God uses to communicate truth.

REASON

God wants us to use our minds—and to use them well.

Let me get a little technical: Reason is the human capacity and inclination toward rational, logical, and analytical thought. For example, if I met a gentleman walking on crutches and wearing a hat that said "Ski Aspen," I would probably draw the following conclusions. First, I would think that his leg was broken. Second, I would think he broke his leg while skiing. I would not need to have read a book to draw such conclusions. And I would not need to be really smart to do so. I would simply employ the rational way of thinking that we are all born with. If someone has a cast on his leg, this normally means his leg is broken. If his leg is broken, there is a cause for its breaking (i.e., it did not break on its own). This is not rocket science.

In the Christian life, God has given you the ability to think, reason, and draw conclusions. Your abilities in this area are by no means perfect, but they are abilities nonetheless. God created you with a mind to think for a reason. He wants you to be reasonable! Reason or rationality is another authority in your life and a valid source for information about God. It is not a Christian virtue to go around believing things that don't make sense. You are not supposed to check your brains at the door once you become a Christian. God expects you to think and to think well.

Here's another illustration. When the Israelites were worshiping gods that they made out of the wood from trees, using half the wood for idols and the other half for their fire, God chastises them for their irrationality. Translation: *they were not thinking well.*

No one considers [stops to think], nor is there knowledge or discernment to say, "Half of it I burned in the fire; I also baked bread on its coals; I roasted meat and have eaten. And shall I make the rest of it an abomination? Shall I fall down before a block of wood?" (Isa. 44:19)

It was irrational for the Israelites to worship blocks of wood, and God calls them on this. God wants and expects you to use your brain.

But reason is not perfect. It can go bad. We can misuse it or misinterpret the data. More often than not, we lack data because we don't have access to all the information and make assumptions. For example, I think I could reasonably conclude that the gentleman in the cast broke his leg while skiing. But what if I was missing some information or misinterpreting what I saw? What if the leg was not broken? What if it was a torn ACL from a car accident? What if the hat was the man's brother's, and he had not been to Aspen at all? All of these things are possible and demonstrate the limits of reason. Only those with all the information are able to draw perfectly sound conclusions. And people, being limited, don't normally have all the information.

The Bible, on the other hand, being the Word of God, is never lacking in perspective. Everything it speaks about, it does so with complete truthfulness and accuracy.

EXPERIENCE

God wants to meet you in your experience. As a disciple, you can see God's hand in the agency of life. But be careful!

The best way to explain experience is to describe it as information that comes through direct encounter, participation, or observation. As a Christian, you should expect to encounter God in your life. While the Bible plainly says that you will not see him with your eyes (1 Pet. 1:8), this does not mean that he is not active. Every day you are to pray for direction and guidance. You might pray for "open doors" and "closed doors." For example, the Bible may tell you nothing beyond general stewardship principles about whether to take this job or that, or to buy this house or that, but you don't want to discount God's desire to guide you through such endeavors. God will open doors through your experience, and he will close doors through your experience.

I am married with four kids. Before my wife and I met many years ago, I was not looking through the Bible to find out what the name of Michael Patton's wife would be. Nevertheless, I did pray that God would prepare a wife for me and that he would guide me to her through the mundane travels of life. Now that I am married, I am fully confident that God did guide me. Through subtle but definite movements, God will often guide and direct your life through experience.

Remember, God is a God of history. He did not finish writing the Bible and go AWOL. When the last book of the Bible was complete, God did not turn into a cheerleader on the sidelines of history. He is still involved. You should expect that he hears your prayers and moves in time, accomplishing his will through you.

But experience, like reason, can be misinterpreted and abused. Experience can be dangerous. Sometimes we can try to manipulate the will of God by making our experience say something that may be at odds with God's will. Allow me to use an extreme example. I could have prayed to God while thinking about whether I should marry Kristie, "Dear God, if Kristie is the one I should marry, make a car come down the street next. If she is not the one, make it a truck." Don't go there. God cannot be manipulated in such a way. You are to always be looking for his movements in your life, but don't force them.

Again, the Bible is in authority over our experience. If

our experience says one thing and the Bible says another, the Bible wins.

EMOTIONS

God wants to speak to your heart. He loves emotions. After all, he created them. Look for God in the depths of your heart.

Emotions are subjectively experienced psychological feelings. We often look down on emotions as a second-rate form of guidance. We talk about not being "too emotional" when we make decisions. It is good to be cautious, but we don't want to dismiss emotions too quickly. God will move through them. For example, the Bible tells us that one of the primary functions of the Holy Spirit is to *convict* us of sin (John 16:7–8). Conviction is an emotion from God that we dare not ignore. The Bible also talks about the *peace* of God that comes into our lives that passes all understanding (Phil. 4:7). Emotions are powerful, and I encourage you to invite God to comfort and guide you through them.

But emotions can be misleading. I have a Christian friend who just fell in love with his "soul mate." However, his so-called soul mate is not a Christian. The Bible is clear that Christians are not to marry unbelievers (2 Cor. 6:14). My friend's emotions are conflicting with the Bible. He thinks the love he has for this woman is from God and is guiding him to marry her. But Scripture says something different. The Bible should always win.

I have another friend who does not "feel" God's presence in his life. He does not "feel" as if God loves him. His depression and inability to be happy, for him, are proof of God's absence. Again, emotions are telling him something that is not true. They can do that. They do it all the time with me. We must be careful.

I want you to welcome God to talk to you through your emotions, but your emotions are not the final arbiter of truth. The Bible is the final arbiter of truth and has authority over your emotions. If your emotions go left (i.e., God does not love me) and the Bible goes right (i.e., God does love me), always go right.

TRADITION

Finally, we need to look at tradition. We should look to the past to find wisdom for the present.

The best way to describe tradition is "those who have gone before us." In the Christian faith, we have a heritage. The church is made up of more than your local assembly meeting in the building on the corner. It is more than all the Christians who are living around the world. The church is made up of all of those who have trusted in Christ, both living *and dead*. God the Holy Spirit has led and guided a multitude of saints that have gone before us. Their common confession through their deeds and beliefs forms an authority for the Christian life. Their witness builds a foundation of truth and beckons us to follow them.

A man once came to me and pointed to a particular portion of Scripture. He told me that he believed that the Holy Spirit had given him an understanding of this particular passage the night before. As he told me about his interpretation, I realized one problem: no Christian before him had ever interpreted the passage that way. His interpretation was completely outside the great Christian tradition that has been held for the last two thousand years. If his belief was true, then multitudes of Christians who had come before him had missed it, even though they were being led by the same Spirit as he supposedly was. This should give us pause. In fact, it should scare us a bit. Look into tradition. Become a student of the great believers of the past. Read biographies on them. Read their works (we have lots of them). Let them become close friends.

However, tradition is not perfect. People who have gone before us have misread and manipulated the Scriptures. While tradition stands guard beside the Scriptures, it is always judged ultimately *by* the Scriptures. In other words, rightly interpreted Scripture affirms or corrects all traditions. You must look to the community of God, both living and dead, for guidance. You must stand in fear of coming up with something "new." However, you must never place tradition above Scripture.

SOLA SCRIPTURA

We have many sources of authority in our lives. In addition to emotions, experience, reason, and tradition, we also have pastors, governments, and parents. These are all from God. All of them carry varying degrees of authority. However, none of them are as authoritative as Scripture. Scripture is your final authority in all things. When it speaks clearly, it does not matter what your emotions say, it does not matter what your reason says, and it does not matter what the government says. God's Word is final.

In the book of Acts, shortly after Christ ascended into heaven, the apostles were taken into custody by the governing authority in their land. They were told to quit preaching about Christ or suffer the legal consequences. Here is what they said:

> But Peter and John answered them, "Whether it is right
> in the sight of God to listen to you rather than to God,

you must judge, for we cannot but speak of what we have seen and heard." (Acts 4:19–20)

We also know that the Christians in Berea fact-checked the apostle Paul against the Scriptures, and they were commended for it!

The brothers immediately sent Paul and Silas away by night to Berea, and when they arrived they went into the Jewish synagogue. Now these Jews were more noble than those in Thessalonica; they received the word with all eagerness, *examining the Scriptures daily to see if these things were so*. (Acts 17:10–11)

CONCLUSION

When I went to my dad for permission to go to my friend's house, I was trying to circumvent the word of my mother. I was attempting to manipulate authorities in order to get *my* way. If you allow yourself this liberty in the Christian life, you will consistently fall on your face, outside of the will of God. Most importantly, you will be a fish out of water. As a believer in Christ, the best place you can be is under the authority of the One who loves you and made you. He knows what is best. Why would we seek anything else?

As a Christian disciple, you must build a respect for all the authorities that God has given. Yes, God is the ultimate authority in your life, but the ultimate way in which God has chosen to communicate this authority is through the Scriptures. This is why as a Christian you must read, meditate on, and study the Bible as often as you are able (more on this later). It is indispensable for Christian discipleship.

DISCUSSION QUESTIONS

1. How has your understanding of Christian authority grown?
2. In what ways do you think emotions could conflict or support the Bible? Give examples.
3. Why should we trust Scripture over experience? Give examples of where experience might *support* the Bible.
4. Why is tradition dangerous *and* wonderful? Give examples outside of Christianity, too.
5. If Scripture seems to come in conflict with modern scientific opinion, what should we do? Give examples.

ADDITIONAL DISCIPLESHIP TRAINING

The Discipleship Program, Credo House Ministries

A General Introduction to the Bible, Norman L. Geisler and William E. Nix

Sola Scriptura: The Protestant Position on the Bible, Joel R. Beeke et. al.

2

Man

This chapter is about man and sin. I am very acquainted with each. My job is to help you get to know yourself through the eyes of God.

Let's start with a history lesson.

During the time of the Enlightenment of the seventeenth century, the Western world "woke up" to a startling realization. Man (re)discovered that he was filled with potential. Having had his abilities, from his perspective, suppressed for over a thousand years, man took on a banner of hope. Advancements in technology, science, and medicine propelled the dreams of what man could be if he were just given the opportunity to discover and set his intellect free. For eighteenth-century philosopher Immanuel Kant, the Enlightenment was "mankind's final coming of age, the emancipation of the human consciousness from an immature state of ignorance and error." The dignity of man was emancipated from the authoritarian structures of religious institutionalism, tradition, archaic morality, and, yes, the Bible. We shed our need of God. Man was now the captain of his fate and the master of his soul. Thus, the dignity of man was "discovered." As I have often heard Chuck Swindoll put it, we thought we were "something on a stick."

However, things did not go as well as we had hoped. Yes, there were and continue to be great advancements in science and technology. But continued death, poverty, hunger, holocaust, and war demonstrate that the "great emancipation" did not rescue man from his greatest problem: sin. The discoveries of the vastness of the universe only served to make us shrink in our confidence in knowledge. The theory of evolution suggested that man was evolving into a higher life form, which was supposed to be better than the previous life form. However, pride, selfishness, hate, rape, murder, and all forms of what we call "inhumanity" continue to excel. Besides all this, without God in the picture, who defines what "better" is? Who defines morality? Who has the authority to define what it means to be "enlightened" or evolved? In the end, man (re) discovered both his dignity *and* his sin.

DIGNITY

Please understand, in a very real sense, man, as God created him, is very good. *You* are very good. This idea is not just something from the enlightenment philosophers; it's from the Bible itself. The first book of the Bible is Genesis. Genesis means "starting" or "beginning." Though the book covers thousands of years of history, its first few chapters are about the creation of all things, with a special emphasis on man. Having accounted for God's creation of the earth, stars, sun, moon, sky, sea, and all the animals in twenty-five short verses, there is a dramatic pause in the narrative as something different is about to take place. "*Then* God said . . ." This is the introduction to the creation of man. The creation of everything else had been going at breakneck speed. But what is about to take place is different in so many ways. While everything God created was special and miraculous, the creation of man demanded a different sort of attention. We pick up here in this drama:

> Then God said, "Let us make man in our image, after our likeness. And let them have dominion over the fish of the sea and over the birds of the heavens and over the livestock and over all the earth and over every creeping thing that creeps on the earth."

> So God created man in his own image,
> in the image of God he created him;
> male and female he created them. (Gen. 1:26–27)

Nothing else in all of creation is like humanity. Man alone is said to be created in the "image of God." Notice the three-fold repetition of the phrase "in [God's] image." Both male and female carry this dignity. Out of all the details that God could have given about the "hows" of creation (questions we often want answered first), he gives us the "what" of creation. We alone are image bearers of the eternal God. This means that you are like God. Amazing!

David, in the Psalms, scratches his head and ponders this wonder: "What is man that you are mindful of him, and the son of man that you care for him? Yet you made him a little lower than the heavenly beings and crowned him with glory and honor" (Ps. 8:4–5).

How are you like God? Good question. Theologians (those guys who study the Bible *a lot*) don't know *exactly* what it means to be in the "image of God." It could include volition, responsibility, morality, spirituality, dominionality, or rationality. It probably is a combination of all of these. It is not that the rest of the animal kingdom doesn't have these to some degree; it is just that man is special, possessing them to a much greater degree.

The point is that any study of the biblical view of man must include a central focus on humanity's dignity as image bearers of God. God wants you to know that you are *the* central part of the creation of the universe. Everything else, all the stars and galaxies, all the mysterious life teeming in the oceans, all the beauty of the plants, trees, and mountains, and all of the wonders of the world are backup music to the creation of the woman and the man. I know it might sound like a cliché, but you are special. No matter what your race, nationality, age, or IQ, you are created in God's image. As such, you bear incredible dignity.

FALL

I wish our creation as image bearers of God were the end of the story, but it is not. There is a B-side to this record. And the B-side is not good. Man is in the image of God, yes. Man is dignified just by virtue of being a human, yes. We are the "apple of God's eye," yes. But something bad happened and it affects us all: sin entered the picture.

After God created his masterpiece, he placed them in a garden called Eden (it was really more like an orchard). He crowned man's dignity with responsibility, giving humanity the opportunity to act as God's vice-regent here on earth. Man was to rule over everything God had created. God also gave man a warning:

And the LORD God commanded the man, saying, "You may surely eat of every tree of the garden, *but of the tree of the knowledge of good and evil you shall not eat,* for in the day that you eat of it you shall surely die." (Gen. 2:16–17)

God gave this command to man in order to allow him to freely choose to obey or not obey. God did not want to force his love and acceptance on man, so he gave him opportunity to rebel. Sure enough, man rebelled. He disobeyed God's command and fell into sin. Here is how the narrative goes:

Now the serpent was more crafty than any other beast of the field that the LORD God had made. He said to the woman, "Did God actually say, 'You shall not eat of any tree in the garden'?" And the woman said to the serpent, "We may eat of the fruit of the trees in the garden, but God said, 'You shall not eat of the fruit of the tree that is in the midst of the garden, neither shall you touch it, lest you die.'" But the serpent said to the woman, "You will not surely die. For God knows that when you eat of it your eyes will be opened, and you will be like God, knowing good and evil." So when the woman saw that the tree was good for food, and that it was a delight to the eyes, and that the tree was to be desired to make one wise, she took of its fruit and ate, and she also gave some to her husband who was with her, and he ate. Then the eyes of both were opened, and they knew that they were naked. And they sewed fig leaves together and made themselves loincloths. (Gen. 3:1–7)

We cannot overstate the importance of what happened here. This event is incredibly significant and alters the progress of all of creation. We call this event *the fall*. As you will see, the fall has affected every man who has been born since. The dignity that man has as image bearers of God is still present, but it is infected with sin. Oh, no. There is that word: *sin*.

SIN

Sin is not a popular word, but it is impossible to be a Christian disciple without believing deeply in its reality. The Bible clearly says that *every* human has sinned: "All have sinned and fall short of the glory of God" (Rom. 3:23).

The "all" here includes you.

Sin means, among other things, to "miss the mark." It has the idea of overstepping boundaries. In short, sin is disobedience and rebellion against God. I don't know if you have ever been involved in a national rebellion. I imagine not. A national rebellion is when people of a country seek to overthrow the leadership of that country. When we talk about sin, we are talking about humanity's attempt to overthrow God. It's a coup d'état against the divine, if you will. In one way or another, we don't like God's program, so we attempt to replace him as leader. The replacement is always ourselves.

Sin is falling short of God's perfection. God is perfect in every way. When we fail to live up to his perfections—when we disobey—we have set ourselves up as king and raised our own flag of supremacy over his, saying our ways are better than his. It is not as though we are trying to reach something that we are not tall enough to reach. It is that we *willfully* turn our backs on God's plan. This is what happened when Adam and Eve decided that their judgment to eat the forbidden fruit was superior to that of God's.

IMPUTED SIN

When Adam and Eve sinned, God could have done one of two things. He could have left man to his rebellious fate, the whole race being condemned to live a life of rebellion with God, or he could have chosen to "fix" what was broken. If he had chosen the first option, man would be hopeless and God would still be righteous. But God, due to his great love, chose the second way. God chose to redeem man. This redemption would need to both provide forgiveness of sins and allow God to remain righteous. God immediately initiated his plan to redeem the world through the sacrifice of his Son (Gen. 3:15). He started to fix what man broke and replace the flag of man with his own. Man rebelled, but God loved.

When Adam sinned, the entire race of man was condemned with him. This is often referred to as "imputed sin." *Imputed* is an accounting term. It is appropriate because we are all born with a sin debt. This debt was created in Eden. It is a debt that every human, including you, has inherited directly from Adam and Eve.

Notice what Paul says: "Therefore, as one trespass led to condemnation for all men, so one act of righteousness leads to justification and life for all men. For as by the one man's disobedience the many were made sinners, so by the one man's obedience the many will be made righteous" (Rom. 5:18–19). The one sin that led to condemnation (debt/imputation) for all men was the sin of Adam. You and I are born into a condemned human race.

The doctrine of imputed sin, while shared by both Catholics and Protestants (generally speaking), is rejected by Eastern Orthodox. However, we all agree about "inherited sin."

INHERITED SIN

It has often been said that our sinful nature is the primary Christian doctrine that can be empirically (with our eyes) proved. In other words, it does not take long to recognize our tendency to rebel. We are prone to selfishness, laziness, hate, deception, sexual perversion, and anger. Just think about your own life for ten seconds and you will see what I mean. Why is this? The answer is found in a Christian doctrine called *inherited sin*. Just as you inherit certain traits from your parents (i.e., eye color, height, and skin color), you also inherit a tendency to rebel against God.

The best way to think of inherited sin is to see it as a spiritual infection. This infection, like a virus, spreads to all mankind. We are born with a sinful *inclination* or disposition. Just as you are born with a hunger for food, you are also born with a hunger for sin. We are born rebels. We can't help but sin. It's in our nature. Listen to the words of the psalmist: "Behold, I was brought forth in iniquity, and in sin did my mother conceive me" (Ps. 51:5).

Paul says that we are rebels "by nature": "Among whom we all once lived in the passions of our flesh, carrying out the desires of the body and the mind, and were *by nature* children of wrath, like the rest of mankind" (Eph. 2:3).

And Jeremiah says we are hopeless in our condition: "Can the Ethiopian change his skin or the leopard his spots? Then also you can do good who are accustomed to do evil" (Jer. 13:23).

Just as we cannot change our genetics, the fall has infected us in such a way that we cannot change our sinful disposition.

We used an accounting term earlier. Let's expand on that here. Not only are you born with a massive debt in your bank account (one so large that it could never be paid off), you are also born with a spending habit. You are in debt, and you, from the moment you are born, continually make that debt greater.

Man was created good. *Everything* that God creates is good. You are in God's image. You are *still* in God's image (James 3:9). But this image has been tainted, infected, and marred by sin. As a Christian disciple, you must come to a firm conclusion about your dignity *and* depravity. Your dignity is the result of God's creative genius. Your depravity is a result of your sin. While there are good things that people do from a human standpoint (i.e., love their children, help the poor, stay off drugs), from the standpoint of our relationship with God, we are born rebels. Outside of God's grace and mercy, there is no one who does good.

You must have a high view of humanity with respect to God's creation, but a low view of humanity with respect to our standing before a perfect God. Therefore, pride and the Christian disciple do not mix.

Romans 3:10–20, perhaps more than any other passage, provides us with the most scathing understanding of where we stand. Allow me some license here as I make this passage very personal.

> You are not righteous, no one is;
>> You don't understand.
>> You don't seek for God;
> You have turned aside and become useless like
>> everyone else.
>> You do not do any good.
>> There is not even one who does.
> Your throat is an open grave.
>> With your tongue you always lie.
> The poison of asps is under your lips.
>> Your mouth is full of cursing and bitterness.
> Your feet are swift to shed blood.
>> Destruction and misery are in your path.
> The path of peace you have not known.
>> There is no fear of God before your eyes.

Now we know that whatever the law says, it speaks to those who are under the law, that your mouth may be closed, and all the world may become accountable to God; because all the good works you can try to do will not justify you in his sight. The rules were given so that you would know you cannot keep them. (AT)

Do you get it? Dignity and depravity. Not evolution, but devolution. Do you see our hopeless condition? Do you recognize that without God's grace through Jesus Christ, we are helpless, hopeless, and without purpose? The Christian disciple must realize how sinful he or she really is in order to receive God's mercy. You don't just *kinda* need God's help. God says we are all absolutely lost without it.

DISCUSSION QUESTIONS

1. Why do you think God created man?
2. How should the reality that man, believer and unbeliever alike, carries the image of God affect the way we treat one another?
3. Why do you think Adam sinned?
4. Man has an inclination toward sin from birth. Describe ways we see this inclination in children.
5. If man is truly dead with no ability to come to God on our own, how are we able to come to him?
6. Name some of the sins that you struggle with.

ADDITIONAL DISCIPLESHIP TRAINING

The Discipleship Program, Credo House Ministries

Humanity and Sin, part 4 of The Theology Program, Credo House Ministries

Not the Way It's Supposed to Be: A Breviary of Sin, Cornelius Plantinga Jr.

Willing to Believe: The Controversy over Free Will, R. C. Sproul

3

God

One of my first jobs was selling cars at a Mitsubishi dealership. I got the job through some connections from my dad. I had never sold anything before and was not sure what to expect. But, as is the case with many types of car dealers, they didn't care too much. As long as I was willing to take a chance with them, they were willing to take a chance with me.

It was my first day and my first customer. "Michael," the manager said, "You've got point. Those people are yours. Go get 'em." It was then that I realized I didn't know the first thing about the cars. Sure, I knew their names, their prices, and where to find the keys to take customers on a test-drive, but what if they asked questions? What if they asked if the car was fuel injected? What if they asked if it had disc brakes? What if they asked about the cylinders, spark plugs, transmission, or gas pump? I thought I could just wing it, but I knew the right person would make me look like a buffoon. I had no business selling *any* type of car.

Multiply that feeling of inadequacy by one billion, and you will see how I feel about writing this chapter. Intimidation, fear, mystery, and all sorts of "buffoonness" are my claim. "Hey,

Michael, you got point. Go tell these people about God! Oh, and don't forget to talk about the Trinity." Yeah, right.

Cars, to me, are mysterious. However, one can spend some time and eventually alleviate themselves of all ignorance. God, *to all people*, is mysterious. We are completely dependent upon him to introduce himself to us.

INEFFABILITY: CAN WE KNOW ABOUT GOD?

I think it's best to put ourselves in place right off the bat. God is infinite; we are finite. God is unlimited; we are limited. God's nature, knowledge, and power know no bounds; we have trouble learning about cars!

I recently watched a clip on the Internet that showed the expanse of our universe. It started with a person in a park in Florida. It then zoomed out ten meters. The rest of the show zoomed out further and further in multiples of ten. It passed the moon, the sun, our solar system, and our galaxy. (Did you know that the closest star to us besides the sun is 4.24 light years away? Light travels at 186,000 miles per second. Per *second*! Even at this speed, it would take over four years to get to the first star in *our* galaxy. And there are about 100 billion stars in our galaxy!) Passing the Milky Way, after hundreds of thousands of light years, we finally pass the nearest galaxy. Yes, that is right, we are only one galaxy among many. In fact, eventually, we would encounter hundreds of billions of galaxies! Where does it end? We don't know. In fact, we don't even know how to define "end." New discoveries make us shrink and cower in amazement. The discoveries are real and true, but they serve only to make us see how small we are.

When we talk about God, the universe is a good illustration. In fact, I think that is why God made it so vast and incomprehensible. And God is infinitely greater than our universe! There are many things we can understand about him, so long as he chooses to reveal himself, but we will never look him eye to eye. We should never be arrogant enough to think we can figure him out *or even any one thing about him.* Any study of God, I believe, must start with his infinite nature and our inability to independently understand him. We call this God's "ineffability." Things that are ineffable are beyond our ability to speak about or understand.

However, we must not make an error and say that he is so great, we cannot come to know him at all. Or that his nature is so infinite that he cannot communicate himself to finite people. It would be like saying, "God is so powerful that he can't tell us about himself." This would make no sense. If he is so powerful, he should be powerful enough to tell us *some* things about himself! We can understand exactly as much as he desires us to understand about him.

Notice what God says in Jeremiah:

> Thus says the LORD: "Let not the wise man boast in his wisdom, let not the mighty man boast in his might, let not the rich man boast in his riches, but let him who boasts boast in this, that he understands and knows me." (Jer. 9:23–24)

You are able to boast about one thing: that you understand and know God. It seems clear that we can come to understand God, at least to the degree that he has revealed himself. An old dictum is appropriate here: "While we cannot come to know God *fully*, we can come to know him *truly*." Why all of this? Because I want you to know that if God wants you to know about him, even though he is infinite, you can understand him! Why? Because he is *that* powerful. It's great news!

ATTRIBUTES OF GOD

Theologians talk about the "attributes" of God. Attributes are characteristics. Take, for example, the desk I have in my office. It has many attributes. It is made of wood. It is painted black. It has four legs, a flat counter surface, and three drawers. Now, some of these attributes are essential to this desk being a desk and some are not. For example, a desk must have a counter surface, right? Without a counter surface, it is, by definition, not a desk. It must also be made of a solid substance. If it were made of water, it would not qualify. However, some characteristics are nonessential but are nevertheless a part of my desk. Its "blackness" is not an essential desk characteristic, but it is, nonetheless, an attribute of *my* desk. As well, while my desk has three drawers, it is not essential for a desk to have *any* drawers.

(Getting too philosophical? Maybe, but I promise it will be worth it.)

When it comes to God, certain attributes are necessary qualifications to being God and certain ones are not necessary, even though he still possesses them. That is why I have divided my short list of attributes into "essential" and "nonessential" attributes.

Essential Attributes

Eternity: God is eternal. This does not simply mean that no matter how far back or how far forward in time you go, God is there. It means that God *transcends* time. He is above and beyond time. He created time, space, and matter all at once, out of nothing (a doctrine we call "creation *ex nihilo*"). God's essence does not exist in time. While God *acts* within time, his essence exists in an "eternal now." Mind blown? We're just getting started! Here are some Scriptures that speak to this attribute, but much of our understanding of God's eternality comes from what he has revealed in nature.

> Before the mountains were brought forth,
>> or ever you had formed the earth and the world,
>> from everlasting to everlasting you are God. (Ps. 90:2)

> But do not overlook this one fact, beloved, that with the Lord one day is as a thousand years, and a thousand years as one day. (2 Pet. 3:8)

Aseity: God is *a se*. This means God is "of himself." Simply put: God is not dependent on anything. You and I are not *a se*. We are not "of ourselves." You had nothing to do with your birth. You have to depend on food, air, temperature, and a thousand other factors that help you live and breathe. God depends on nothing. He needs nothing. He does not even need us. He is completely self-dependent.

Notice in Psalm 50 that God expresses that he does not even need our worship:

> For every beast of the forest is mine,
>> the cattle on a thousand hills.
> I know all the birds of the hills,
>> and all that moves in the field is mine.
> If I were hungry, I would not tell you,
>> for the world and its fullness are mine.
>>> (Ps. 50:10–12)

Ponder that: The God you serve does not need you in any way, but he does desire a relationship with you. Amazing!

Omnipresence: God is everywhere. The best way to think of

this is that there is no place that is outside of God's immediate presence. Wherever you go in the universe, you are in God's sight. Listen to this:

> Where shall I go from your Spirit?
>> Or where shall I flee from your presence?
> If I ascend to heaven, you are there!
>> If I make my bed in Sheol, you are there!
> If I take the wings of the morning
>> and dwell in the uttermost parts of the sea,
> even there your hand shall lead me,
>> and your right hand shall hold me.
> If I say, "Surely the darkness shall cover me,
>> and the light about me be night,"
> even the darkness is not dark to you;
>> the night is bright as the day,
>> for darkness is as light with you. (Ps. 139:7–12)

Take comfort in knowing that God hears you and sees you no better in a church than where you are right now.

Omniscience: God knows everything. God knows the past, present, and future, exhaustively. He even knows your thoughts before you have them. Advancements in technology are simply God's daily allowance to us. Of all the hundreds of billions of stars and galaxies, God is perfectly aware of every one, and even names them all. God's knowledge is perfect; he even knows our hidden motives:

> Lift up your eyes on high and see:
>> who created these?
> He who brings out their host by number,
>> calling them all by name,
> by the greatness of his might,

and because he is strong in power
not one is missing. (Isa. 40:26)

Even before a word is on my tongue,
   behold, O Lᴏʀᴅ, you know it altogether. (Ps. 139:4)

Search me, O God, and know my heart!
   Try me and know my thoughts!
And see if there be any grievous way in me,
   and lead me in the way everlasting! (Ps. 139:23–24)

While it is a scary thing for someone to know your heart and read your thoughts, it is a wonderful thing to have the gracious God of the universe know us in such an intimate way and still love us!

Omnipotence: God has unlimited power. In Scripture, in order to dignify God above all other gods, he is often called the "Almighty." While people and things have "might," no one has *all*-might. God alone is almighty. There is nothing too difficult for him. The only things God can't do are things that are inconsistent with his character. For example, God cannot sin. He cannot lie. He cannot cease to be God. And he cannot make a rock so big he can't pick it up. In other words, God can do all things that are logically possible.

Is anything too hard for the Lᴏʀᴅ? (Gen. 18:14)

I know that you can do all things,
   and that no purpose of yours can be thwarted.
      (Job 42:2)

Hallelujah! For the Lord our God the Almighty reigns. (Rev. 19:6)

In times of difficulty, you can have hope knowing that the greatest being in the universe has your back.

Sovereignty: God is in control over *everything*. There is not a maverick molecule in the universe. He answers to no one other than himself. He has no boss. The buck stops with him. All things, good and evil, happen according to his permissive will. This does not mean that he likes all things that happen, but we must understand that everything must pass by his desk for approval.

> In him we have obtained an inheritance, having been predestined according to the purpose of him who works all things according to the counsel of his will. (Eph. 1:11)

> At the end of the days I, Nebuchadnezzar, lifted my eyes to heaven, and my reason returned to me, and I blessed the Most High, and praised and honored him who lives forever,
>
>> for his dominion is an everlasting dominion,
>>> and his kingdom endures from generation to generation;
>> all the inhabitants of the earth are accounted as nothing,
>>> and he does according to his will among the host of heaven
>>> and among the inhabitants of the earth;
>> and none can stay his hand
>>> or say to him, "What have you done?"
>>> (Dan. 4:34–35)

We will deal with God's sovereignty and its relation to the problem of pain in a later chapter. But I want you to pause and think deeply about the implications of God's sovereignty in your life.

Nonessential Attributes

Grace: God is a God of grace. Grace means "gift." It often carries the idea of stooping, as when a king stoops to bless a commoner who does not deserve it. Grace gives us what we don't deserve. God is gracious. Grace is built into his very nature. He stoops to sinners, giving us gifts and love even though we don't deserve them.

> But if it is by grace, it is no longer on the basis of works; otherwise grace would no longer be grace. (Rom. 11:6)

> For by grace you have been saved through faith. And this is not your own doing; it is the gift of God, not a result of works, so that no one may boast. (Eph. 2:8–9)

> For the grace of God has appeared, bringing salvation for all people. (Titus 2:11)

The hardest thing in the Christian life is to accept God's grace. Believe me, I know. Our sin nature does whatever it can to keep its pride, but you must learn that the very breath you have is due to his stooping. Saturate yourself in grace starting right now.

Love: God is love. Love is not merely a compassionate feeling for someone (though it does include this), but a disposition that continually expresses itself through acts of mercy, grace, forgiveness, and kindness. God's love continually seeks us and is the motivation behind Jesus's going to the cross.

> For God so loved the world, that he gave his only Son, that whoever believes in him should not perish but have eternal life. (John 3:16)

> So we have come to know and to believe the love that God has for us. God is love, and whoever abides in love abides in God, and God abides in him. (1 John 4:16)

Righteousness: God is morally perfect. Not only this, but he is a perfectly just judge. He hates sin. He will never leave sin unpunished. He can't. As a disciple, you must learn to balance the love and grace of God with the righteousness of God. Fail to do this, and you will fail to get the Christian message of the cross. God sent his Son to die for us not only because of his love but because his eternal righteous indignation toward sin and evil demanded punishment. Because of God's love, in grace he sent his Son to satisfy his *own* righteousness.

> Keeping steadfast love for thousands, forgiving iniquity and transgression and sin, but who will by no means clear the guilty. (Ex. 34:7)

And I heard the altar saying,

> "Yes, Lord God the Almighty,
>   true and just are your judgments!" (Rev. 16:7)

You don't have to fear God's judgment, because it was taken care of on the cross. But we should live in fear of his righteousness, because it is why Jesus had to be killed in our place.

TRINITY

Having looked at some of the attributes of God, we now turn briefly to the doctrine of the Trinity. The word *Trinity* cannot be found in Scripture, but the concept is found throughout. The doctrine of the Trinity has been held by all orthodox Christians throughout all of church history. Eastern Orthodox, Roman

Catholic, and historic Protestants have held this doctrine to be a central component of Christian truth that cannot be denied without great sacrifice of the Christian witness. Cults such as Jehovah's Witnesses and Mormons deny the doctrine of the Trinity and have, therefore, fallen into great error. Their denial of the Trinity is the central reason why they are not considered "Christian" traditions, but rather cults.

The doctrine of the Trinity states that we believe in one God who eternally exists in three persons, all of whom are fully God, all of whom are equal.

One God

This is a central confession of monotheism (i.e., belief in one God). We do not believe in three gods. There is and can only be one God. He is the singular source of all things.

Deuteronomy 6:4 states, "Hear, O Israel: The Lord our God, the Lord is one." This is the first "creedal statement" in the Bible. A creedal statement is simply a summary of belief. Central to the confession of the nation of Israel (from which Christianity finds its roots) is a belief in one God.

Three Persons

Progressively revealed throughout the Bible is an understanding of the plurality of God. God is one in essence (the "stuff" of who he is), but the Bible tells us that he is three in person. In other words, the Father is God, Jesus is God, the Holy Spirit is God, but they are not each other. Another way to put it is that we believe in one "what" and three "whos."

John 1:1 states: "In the beginning was the Word, and the Word was with God, and the Word was God." Notice here that Jesus ("the Word") was both *with* God and *was* God. This relationship between the essence and person of God forms the basis for the doctrine of the Trinity. All three members are *with* each other and they *are* God.

Matthew 28:19 says: "Go therefore and make disciples of all nations, baptizing them in the name of the Father and of the Son and of the Holy Spirit." Notice the threefold division of the "name" (singular) of God: Father, Son, and Holy Spirit.

Trinitarian Errors

Modalism is the belief that there is one God who displays himself in three different ways, sometimes as Father, sometimes as Son, sometimes as Holy Spirit. For example, I (Michael) am a son, father, and husband—three roles, one person. But God is three *separate* persons, one essence. Modalism has been universally condemned as heresy (seriously wrong teaching) throughout church history. Modalism destroys the eternal relationship between the Father, Son, and Spirit.

> And when Jesus was baptized, immediately he went up from the water, and behold, the heavens were opened to him, and he saw the Spirit of God descending like a dove and coming to rest on him; and behold, a voice from heaven said, "This is my beloved Son, with whom I am well pleased." (Matt. 3:16–17)

Notice here that we have all three members of the Trinity together in one place, yet they are very distinct. If they were all each other, God has a serious case of multiple personality disorder!

Tritheism is the belief that there are three gods. While it is easy to fall into this error, we must never think of God as three distinct beings. God is one being, three persons.

Ontological (Essential) Subordinationalism is the idea that one member of the Trinity is greater than the others. Sometimes people think that God the Father is the greatest, while God the Son comes in a close second, with God the Holy Spirit placing last. This is error as well. Being one in essence, they all share the same divinity. Therefore, they are equal in everything. This does not mean that they don't take roles that allow for *"functional* subordination." They do, but this does not say anything about their essence. For example, a servant is subordinate to a king, but this does not mean that the king's *nature* is greater than the servant's. It is just his role that is greater. This is why Christ could say, "The Father is greater than I" (John 14:28). He did not mean "greater in essence" (as that would necessarily produce two gods), but greater in role or function.

Bad Illustrations

You may be tempted to use some illustrations to help you understand the doctrine of the Trinity. I know I am. But while I understand how mysterious this doctrine can be, every illustration I have ever heard is an illustration of error. Let me give you some examples of these bad illustrations.

Egg: One egg, three parts: shell, white stuff (it's actually got a name: albumin), and yoke. This actually illustrates tritheism, since each part of the constitution of the egg is separate.

Water: It can be liquid, ice, or steam. This illustrates modalism, since these are merely modes that water can exist in. God is Father, Son, and Spirit always simultaneously.

Shamrock: Three parts, one leaf. This illustrates tritheism, since each part of the leaf is *essentially* distinct from the other. In other words, they don't share in the exact same essence, just similar essences.

Three people: Three people, one human nature. This, again, illustrates tritheism. While three people may share in a like nature, being of the species Homo sapien, they do not share in the *exact* same nature. God the Father, God the Son, and God the Holy Spirit do not share the nature of a species called "deity," they share the *exact* same nature. It's a one-to-one correspondence.

In short, well intentioned illustrations only serve to illustrate heresy.

Here is the best we can do. It is called the Shield of the Trinity.

Fig. 3.1 Shield of the Trinity

We started this chapter talking about the ineffability of God. God is, in so many ways, beyond our comprehension. But take heart! If we could exhaustively comprehend all that God is, then it would not really be God that we comprehended!

As a disciple of Christ, you have been introduced to God. Our job is not to make the ineffable effable, the inscrutable

scrutable, or the unknowable knowable. Our job is to believe what God has revealed because he is trustworthy.

Listen to this carefully: If you are finishing this chapter with some wonder, awe, and maybe even some "buffoonness," that is OK. You have just joined hands with all the great saints of the past. God is infinitely more complex than a car. Yet he has made himself known to you, and you can confidently rejoice in your understanding. Let the revealed mystery of the God we serve bring us to our knees.

DISCUSSION QUESTIONS

1. Why do you think God made the universe so vast?
2. Describe how God is like the universe.
3. God is sovereign over all of creation. How does this comfort you? How might it disturb you?
4. Grace describes God's stooping to us. Why do you think grace is so hard for us to accept?
5. How do you propose that we can start accepting God's grace?
6. Why do you think Christianity has been so universally defined by the doctrine of the Trinity?
7. The doctrine of the Trinity is impossible to understand. How can its ineffability (indescribability) affect the way you worship God?

ADDITIONAL DISCIPLESHIP TRAINING

The Discipleship Program, Credo House Ministries

Knowing God, J. I. Packer

The Knowledge of the Holy, A. W. Tozer

Shared Life: The Trinity and the Fellowship of God's People, Donald Macleod

Trinitarianism, part 3 of The Theology Program, Credo House Ministries

4

Christ

I have so many questions in life. Many involve the day-to-day details that life throws on my desk. But some are more significant.

I have been married for over a decade now. I remember the day I asked Kristie to marry me. We were watching a Dallas Cowboys game at her apartment, and I was scared beyond belief. I had decided the day before that I was going to take the plunge and propose to her. As we sat on the couch together, I could feel my heart about to beat out of my chest. My anxiety was so intense that Kristie, who sat beside me as I had my arm around her, said, "What is wrong with you? Why is your heart beating so hard?" Busted! There was no turning back. After a few more moments of mounting courage, I finally asked her, "Will you marry me?" Why such anxiety? It was a big step, and I did not know what she would say.

It is funny to think about how much our life and future hinges on one question: "Will you marry me?" Had she said no, not only would I have been heartbroken, but so much of who we are now would be different. As I tell couples who come to me to get married, whom you marry is the second most important decision you will ever make in this life. It affects everything. *Everything!* I can't imagine what my life would be like had I not asked that question. I can't imagine my life without my four children, Katelynn, Kylee, Will, and Zach.

However, there is one question that is more important than whom you will marry. *Infinitely* more important. It's a question that Jesus himself asks: "Who do you say that I am?"

As a Christian, you will face many questions, thoughts, struggles, and confusing theological forks in the road. Get ready for it. We don't have *all* the answers. What I have included in this book are the central issues of Christianity. They are those which define the Christian faith and you as a disciple of Christ. They are the things that we believe most. However, "Who do you say that I am?" is the key question of our faith.

While Christ was here on the earth, people who saw him and heard his teaching were often left scratching their heads wondering who this person was. He was doing miracles and teaching with authority beyond anything they were used to or had ever seen. He seemed to be friends with bad people and come down hard on the self-righteous. He was wise, yes. But there was something else about him that transcended anything they had ever known. At one point in his ministry, he asked Peter, one of his twelve students (the twelve disciples, we call them), the central question. The story unfolds in Matthew:

> Now when Jesus came into the district of Caesarea Philippi, he asked his disciples, "Who do people say that the Son of Man is?" And they said, "Some say John the Baptist, others say Elijah, and others Jeremiah or one of the prophets." (Matt. 16:13–14)

You see, the world was already confused and divided about the identity of this obscure character from Nazareth. Most did not know how to place him. Some people thought he was John the Baptist (who had just died a few months before). They knew Jesus was something special, but their opinions varied, usually landing on one of the heroic prophets of old come back to life. Why? Because Jesus seemed to have "insider" knowledge of things that humanity was not privy to. He transcended everything they knew. He was different.

Christ responds in the next verse with part 2 of his pop quiz, asking the key question of all existence: "But who do *you* say that I am?"

That is it! That is the most monumental question ever asked. The importance of the response far outweighs my question to Kristie that Sunday afternoon. Who is Christ? The answer has divided all of history. It has divided mother and father, sister and brother, and father and son. One cannot get this question wrong and have an accepted voice in the presence of God. You cannot be a disciple of Christ and go wrong here.

Who do you say that he is?

JESUS IS FULLY GOD

In the last chapter we walked through the difficult doctrine of the Trinity. There I tried to make it clear that God is both one and three. God is one in essence, three in person. Christ is often referred to as the "second person of the Trinity." Again, this does not mean he is in second place or is second best. It simply means that Christ is one of the three members of what we call the *Godhead*. The most important thing to recognize here is that Christ is fully God. He is not one-third God. He is fully God, sharing in the eternal essence of the Trinity.

Son of God

The most common designation of Christ in the Gospels is "Son of God." In fact, when God the Father (the first person of the Trinity) speaks from heaven at the initiation of Jesus's ministry during his baptism, he identifies Jesus as such:

> And when Jesus was baptized, immediately he went up from the water, and behold, the heavens were opened to him, and he saw the Spirit of God descending like a dove and coming to rest on him; and behold, a voice from heaven said, "This is my beloved Son, with whom I am well pleased." (Matt. 3:16–17)

To be the "son of God" speaks of Christ's personal and intimate relationship to the Father *and* his relationship to the Father's essence. The Father-Son analogy must be kept within these confines. For if Christ is eternally God, he was not, as is the case with human father-son relationships, brought into existence by the Father. He is eternal. Yet he is God the Father's Son. This expresses a unique relationship between the first and second persons of the Trinity, but it also communicates a shared nature.

The Christ

When Christ put Peter on the spot and asked, "Who do *you* say that I am?" Peter's answer was two-fold: "You are the Christ, the Son of the living God" (Matt. 16:16). It may surprise you to learn that this term "Christ" is not Jesus's last name. It is a title equivalent to the Hebrew "Messiah." The concept of the Messiah goes all the way back to the book of Genesis.

Just after Adam and Eve disobeyed God, God pronounced a curse upon them and the Serpent. At the cursing of the Serpent, we get our first hint of what the Messiah will do. God said to the Serpent: "I will put enmity between you and the woman [Eve], and between your offspring and her offspring; he shall bruise your head, and you shall bruise his heel" (Gen. 3:15). This passage is often referred to as the *protoevangelion* or "first gospel." As confusing as this promise undoubtedly was for Adam and Eve, one thing they knew for sure: a man would come from the woman and crush the works of the Serpent. In other words, the things that were broken there that day would someday be fixed. So, in essence, the Messiah was the one who was going to fix what man broke. How he would do this was, at that time, still a mystery.

Throughout the Old Testament, this promise of a head-crushing fixer became more and more defined. In fact, we could say that the primary purpose for most of the Old Testament is to trace the lineage of the Messiah. He was to be a descendant of Abraham (Gen. 12:3), Isaac (Gen. 17:19), Jacob (Num. 24:17), Judah (Gen. 49:10), Jesse (Isa. 11:10), and David (Jer. 23:5–6). He was to be the prophet of God (Deut. 18:15), who would deliver Israel from oppression through his death and resurrection (Isaiah 53), and who would establish an eternal throne (Isa. 9:7).

He was the hope of Israel and the hope of the entire world. When Christ finally came on the scene, declaring him as the Christ was nothing less than declaring him as the ultimate apex of history. He was the one everyone was waiting for, the Savior, Deliverer, King, Anointed One of God, Messiah.

God

Many times in the New Testament, Christ is explicitly called "God." The most extraordinary place is found in the book of

John: "In the beginning was the Word, and the Word was with God, and the Word was God" (John 1:1).

Christ was the "Word" (i.e., the reason that "all things hold together" [Col. 1:17]). He was God and he was with God. This incredible statement expresses the full deity of Christ along with his distinction from the Father. Jesus was God in essence, but in fellowship with the Father in person. This was so even before anything was ever made.

Listen to what Paul says to the Philippians:

> Have this mind among yourselves, which is yours in Christ Jesus, who, though he was in the form of God, did not count equality with God a thing to be grasped, but emptied himself, by taking the form of a servant, being born in the likeness of men. And being found in human form, he humbled himself by becoming obedient to the point of death, even death on a cross. (Phil. 2:5–8)

Although Christ is equal with God (the Father), he did not try to hold onto this rank. In humility and for the love of mankind, Christ took on a human nature, submitting himself to the weaknesses of man, even to the point of death on a cross. This statement of Paul's would be meaningless if Christ were not fully God.

Consider the following passage from John, where Christ is in a dispute with the Jewish leaders of his day:

> "My sheep hear my voice, and I know them, and they follow me. I give them eternal life, and they will never perish, and no one will snatch them out of my hand. My Father, who has given them to me, is greater than all, and no one is able to snatch them out of the Father's hand. I and the Father are one." The Jews picked up stones again

to stone him. Jesus answered them, "I have shown you many good works from the Father; for which of them are you going to stone me?" The Jews answered him, "It is not for a good work that we are going to stone you but for blasphemy, because you, being a man, make yourself God." (John 10:27–33)

These people knew exactly who Christ was claiming to be, and that is why they eventually killed him.

If you are still wondering whether we are elevating Jesus too high, consider this. Many have rightly said that there are only four options when considering who Christ was; he had to be either a legend, a lunatic, a liar, or Lord. (C. S. Lewis was the first to articulate this idea in such a way. Later writers have recognized and added the "legend" option.) There is no option for Christ to be a cool guy if he was not really God. If he really existed and was only human, he was either a madman or a liar. Notice what he said about himself:

The basis of the final judgment will be man's relationship to him (Matt. 25:31–46).

He speaks of his angels (Matt. 13:41; 16:27; 24:31).

People are commanded to love him more than their own families (Matt. 10:37).

Eternal life depends on belief in him and the Father (John 17:3).

There are blessings for those who are persecuted because of him (Matt. 5:11).

He will say who enters the kingdom of heaven (Matt. 7:21–23).

We are to give up our lives to follow him (Matt. 16:25).

He will repay each person for what he has done (Matt. 16:27–28).

Humans don't say these things about themselves (unless they want to be locked away!). Christ knew who he was, and he asks you, "Who do you say that I am?"

JESUS IS FULLY MAN

While Christ is fully God, we can easily forget that he is also fully man. Christ had to become man in order to redeem man. Notice in the book of John: "And the Word [Jesus] became flesh and dwelt among us, and we have seen his glory, glory as of the only Son from the Father, full of grace and truth" (John 1:14).

Christ became flesh! Think about that. The eternal second person of the Trinity who spoke and brought all of existence into being took on a complete human nature. Not a human nature glowing with the glory of God. Not a human nature surrounded by a legion of angels. Not a human nature that did not leave footprints when he walked. In fact, Jesus was so much a man that the average Joe who came into contact with Christ had no idea that he was in contact with his Creator. Consider: "He was in the world, and the world was made through him, yet the world did not know him" (John 1:10).

Let's return to Philippians 2:

> Have this mind among yourselves, which is yours in Christ Jesus, who, though he was in the form of God, did not count equality with God a thing to be grasped, but emptied himself, by taking the form of a servant, being born in the likeness of men. *And being found in human form, he humbled himself by becoming obedient to the point of death, even death on a cross.* (vv. 5–8)

Jesus was found in human form. Amazing! He ate and drank (Matt. 11:19), had to use the bathroom, got cramps in his stomach, needed to rest (Mark 6:31), fell asleep when tired (Matt. 8:24), cried (John 11:35), grew in knowledge (Luke 2:52), got splinters, needed to bathe, and had to open doors to go inside places. And he did leave footprints in the sand. Christ was every bit as human as you and I.

Why did God become man? Why couldn't God accomplish his purpose of redemption (i.e., fixing what was broken) without having to stoop so low as to become a man?

Simply put, our old representation was tainted. We needed new representation. The race related to Adam (all people other than Christ) was infected with a virus called sin. Therefore, it was condemned. We need a new or "second Adam."

Jesus had to do what the first Adam could not. He had to succeed where Adam failed. He had to live a life as a human and never sin. He had to gain the right to be our representative on the cross. If Christ were not man, man could not be saved. Christ was conceived by the Holy Spirit so that he would not have a fallen sinful nature, but he was also born of a woman so that he would be fully man. "Thus it is written, 'The first man Adam became a living being'; the last Adam became a life-giving spirit" (1 Cor. 15:45). Christ was the "last Adam"!

> Therefore he had to be made like his brothers in every respect, so that he might become a merciful and faithful high priest in the service of God, to make propitiation for the sins of the people. For because he himself has suffered when tempted, he is able to help those who are being tempted. (Heb. 2:17–18)

Christ could come to your aid as a priest (a representative to God for the people) and die on the cross bearing the wrath of God precisely because he is just like you in every way—except for sin. As Paul expressed it: "For there is one God, and there is one mediator between God and men, the man Christ Jesus" (1 Tim. 2:5).

We know that Christ's representation fixed what was broken because of his resurrection (Rom. 1:4). The bodily resurrection of Christ is the stamp of approval upon Christ's mission. It is the "redemption accomplished" act that we can look to with great confidence, knowing that the mission of God to restore his creation is complete. Things got fixed. Since Jesus rose from the grave, we too can be confident that one day we will rise with him. Our bodies will be restored, and sickness, sin, and death will be no more.

This is why Paul says that Christ's resurrection is the essence of the gospel. It is of "first importance."

> Now I would remind you, brothers, of the gospel I preached to you, which you received, in which you stand, and by which you are being saved, if you hold fast to the word I preached to you—unless you believed in vain. For I delivered to you as of first importance what I also received: that Christ died for our sins in accordance with the Scriptures, that he was buried, that he was raised on the third day in accordance with the Scriptures. (1 Cor. 15:1–4)

Read that again, slowly. Memorize it. In one paragraph, we have the gospel (the "good news"). Without the resurrection, nothing is fixed.

WAYS TO GO WRONG WITH CHRIST

Now that we know Christ is both God and man, how do the two relate? Throughout history, as with many other things, the doctrine of who Christ is became articulated through bad ideas. The truths in the Bible are unchanging. But often it takes time for these truths to work themselves out in history. Here are three ways people have gone wrong in their beliefs about Christ's nature.

Nestorianism

Developed by a fifth-century bishop, Nestorianism proposed that Christ is of two natures that formed two persons—in one body. Picture this: the second person of the Trinity, Christ, comes down from heaven and finds some guy named Jesus. He says, "Hello, Jesus. My name is Christ. I was hoping you could help me out and work together with me to save mankind." To which Jesus says, "I don't have anything else on the calendar. Let's do it!"

For the Nestorian, when Christ was here on earth doing things like walking on water, that was his divine person showing through. When he was ignorant of the time of his coming (Matt. 24:36), that was the human person.

The basic problem with Nestorianism is that we fail to have a human representative who is qualified to fix what was broken. What we really have is an unqualified man who is possessed by the divine. In this situation we have neither representation before God nor representation before man.

This is not what we mean when we talk about Christ being the God-man.

Apollinarianism

Another view to throw its hat into the early church ring was Apollinarianism (named after another bishop, Apollinarius of Laodicea). Apollinarius proposed that Christ took on human flesh and displaced the human soul. This would mean Christ was deity surrounded by the skin of a man. In other words, Christ did not have a human soul, just human flesh and bones. Think "God in a bod," and you will be pretty close.

The major problem with Apollinarianism is, as Gregory of Nazianzus made clear in the fourth century, that "what God has not assumed is not healed." In other words, you and I need someone to die for our body *and* soul. If Christ did not have a human soul, then our soul is not saved. Christ had to become everything that we are in order for everything in us to be saved.

This "God in a bod" option is not what we mean when we talk about Christ being the God-man.

Eutychianism

During the fourth and early fifth centuries, one final option was under discussion, but decisively rejected. Eutyches was yet another well-meaning theologian who made this proposal: Christ's humanity was mixed with and swallowed up by his deity. When Christ became man, the divine overwhelmed the man and the distinction of the natures essentially mingled. Human and divine came together and formed a new entity, a "humine."

I hope you can see what the issue with Eutychianism is: there is no such thing as a humine! *A humine could only save other humines.* Therefore, because Christ no longer had a complete human *or* divine nature, no one could be represented!

Solution: Hypostatic Union

The solution comes when we understand that Christ must remain fully divine and fully human. He is not 50/50. He is not 90/10 or even 10/90. He is 100 percent God and 100 percent man. As the definition of Chalcedon, a great historic creed of the Christian faith, put forth in 451: "Christ is very God of very

God and very man of very man." Whereas the Trinity is one nature and three persons, Christ is one person of two natures. This is what we call the *hypostatic union*.

Christ is fully God and fully man. He is in heaven now making intercession for you (i.e., when we do wrong, he says of believers, "I've got these covered. Put them on my tab."). He is the eternal God-man. He is the center of our theology. We are called *Christ*ians, which means we are followers of Christ.

The message of who Christ is is the message that we bring to people. Life presents lots of important questions and issues, not the least of which is whom we marry. But, *who do you say Christ is?* is far and away the most important. As a disciple of Christ, you are a *Christopher*, a "Christ bearer." The God-man Messiah who lived a sinless life, died, rose from the grave, and now stands at the Father's right hand making intercession for you is who you are bearing. He is the center of all things. He *is* Christianity.

Christ asked Peter, "Who do you say that I am?" Peter made the great confession: "You are the Christ, the Son of the living God." After this, Christ said to him, "Blessed are you, Simon Bar-Jonah! For flesh and blood has not revealed this to you, but my Father who is in heaven" (Matt. 16:15–17). With some latitude, I say this to you: "Blessed are you, disciple of Christ. For your trust in and confession of Christ has been given to you by God."

DISCUSSION QUESTIONS

1. The person and work of Christ are the most essential issues of Christianity. The question, *who do you say that I am?* is the most important question ever asked. Why do you believe that God cares so much about your knowledge and relationship with Christ?

2. How many different representations of Christ do you see in the world today? Who does your culture say that he is?

3. Matthew 24:36 says that Christ, while here on earth, did not know the time of his second coming. Though we believe that Christ *could have* known the time of his coming, being God, we believe that he did not know the time of his coming, being man. Why do you think Christ did not access this information?

4. Satan tempted Christ to turn a stone into bread (Luke 4:3). It is not a sin to turn stones into bread. Why do you think Satan was trying to get Jesus to use his divine power to satisfy his hunger? (Hint: had Jesus listened to Satan, humanity would have lost representation.)

5. What do you think of the legend-lunatic-liar-Lord dilemma? How does it help you understand the necessity of thinking deeply about Jesus?

ADDITIONAL DISCIPLESHIP TRAINING

The Person of Christ, Contours of Christian Theology, Donald Macleod

Putting Jesus in His Place: The Case for the Deity of Christ, Robert Bowman, J. Ed Komoszewski

Reinventing Jesus, J. Ed Komoszewski, Dan Wallace, James Sawyer

5

Faith

Each day is filled with choices. Many of those choices are based on habit. I don't necessarily consciously *choose* which way I will drive to work each and every day. Every turn is not a contemplative battle of thinking through the pros and cons of the directions I could take. I have simply driven to work so many times, I can do it without thinking. As well, when I shave, I always start in the same place (the left sideburn) and end in the same place (the left neck). Again, I do this not because that is the best or most well-thought-out way to shave; I shave this way because that is the way I have always done it. Both my drive to work and the way I shave (along with a thousand other things in my life) are done by rote.

I am afraid that when it comes to people's faith in God, things often aren't much different. Why do some people believe in Jesus, others in Allah, and some in no god at all? Why are some people Christians, others Hindus, some Buddhists, and others Jews? Why do some people just barely live out their faith while others are gung-ho crazy about it? There are thousands of different religious beliefs and practices. All of them require some sort of faith. But many people practice their faith just like they practice their drive to work or their shaving—by rote. They simply believe what they believe and do what they do, not because it is well-thought-out, but because this is the way they have always done it.

In this chapter, we are going to talk about faith. We are going to define what true Christian faith is and how you can continually grow it.

THE IMPORTANCE OF FAITH IN THE BIBLE

To say that faith is a concept found in the Bible is about the biggest understatement I could make. From beginning to end, the Bible tells us that faith is what God requires of us. Both in the Old Testament and the New Testament God calls on us to believe in him.

Abraham, the father of the Jewish nation in the Old Testament, was visited by God and told to leave his home and move to a new land:

> Now the LORD said to Abram, "Go from your country and your kindred and your father's house to the land that I will show you. And I will make of you a great nation, and I will bless you and make your name great, so that you will be a blessing. I will bless those who bless you, and him who dishonors you I will curse, and in you all the families of the earth shall be blessed." So Abram went. (Gen. 12:1–4)

Can you imagine this? Abraham was comfortable in his homeland. He was surrounded by all of his friends and family. He probably had many plans. Yet God, out of the blue, told him to leave it all and find greater purpose in him. Abraham left the rote routine of his previous faith and believed God. Later, we are told that this act of faith is what brought about Abraham's righteousness: "And he believed the LORD, and he counted it to him as righteousness" (Gen. 15:6).

An old bumper sticker says, "God said it, I believe it, that settles it." Things are not always so simple, but sometimes they are. Your belief is very important to God.

We find the verb *believe* in the book of John more than in any book in the Bible. There Christ continually says that our relationship to him is based on our belief. Consider some examples:

> But to all who did receive him, *who believed in his name*, he gave the right to become children of God. (John 1:12)

> For God so loved the world, that he gave his only Son, that *whoever believes* in him should not perish but have eternal life. (John 3:16)

> *Whoever believes in him* is not condemned, but whoever does not believe is condemned already, because he has not believed in the name of the only Son of God. (John 3:18)

> Truly, truly, I say to you, whoever hears my word *and believes him who sent me* has eternal life. He does not come into judgment, but has passed from death to life. (John 5:24)

> Jesus said to them, "I am the bread of life; whoever comes to me shall not hunger, *and whoever believes in me* shall never thirst." (John 6:35)

> I told you that you would die in your sins, for *unless you believe that I am he [God]* you will die in your sins. (John 8:24)

> Jesus said to her, "I am the resurrection and the life. *Whoever believes in me*, though he die, yet shall he live." (John 11:25)

Finally, at the end of John's Gospel, John writes:

> Now Jesus did many other signs in the presence of the disciples, which are not written in this book; but these are written so *that you may believe* that Jesus is the Christ, the Son of God, and that *by believing* you may have life in his name. (John 20:30–31)

Notice that it is just by believing that you have life in his name.

The entire New Testament convinces us of the importance of faith in our discipleship. Paul writes:

> For we hold that one is justified by faith apart from works of the law. (Rom. 3:28)

> Therefore, since we have been justified by faith, we have peace with God through our Lord Jesus Christ. (Rom. 5:1)

> For by grace you have been saved through faith. And this is not your own doing; it is the gift of God, not a result of works, so that no one may boast. (Eph. 2:8–9)

Luke records the same truth:

> And he [Jesus] said to the woman, "Your faith has saved you; go in peace." (Luke 7:50)

> And they said, "Believe in the Lord Jesus, and you shall be saved, you and your household." (Acts 16:31)

I could go on and on, but you get the idea. I hope that you are convinced that God desires and requires us to believe.

WHY DOES GOD CARE SO MUCH?

Why does God care so much about being believed? Well, don't you? After all, if you are a trustworthy person, how would you like it if people *didn't* believe you?

When I was a kid, one of my best friends accused me of stealing his Hot Wheels. I assured him over and over again that I didn't steal them, but he just would not believe me. Every time I would try to assure him of my innocence, he would respond, "Yes, you did." Even into our adult lives (and we are still best friends), I bring it up every once in a while: "You know, Jason, I never stole those Hot Wheels." "Yes, you did," he still responds! Though it has become a joke between the two of us, it is still frustrating. Why? Because I desire to be believed. I *deserve* to be believed. I didn't take them! When it comes to God our father, how much more does he desire to be believed by his children? When it comes to the God of the universe, how much more does he *deserve* to be believed? After all, if anyone is in the know, it is him.

That is why it is so important for you to believe God continually. You see, when you became a Christian, you did not just believe God for one thing he said (i.e., that Jesus died for your sins and rose from the grave). You became a believer in *everything* God says. You are a believer. Your life is characterized by continually believing God.

FOUR TYPES OF FAITH

We can define faith in four different ways. It is incredibly important that you, as a child of God, don't go wrong here.

1. Faith as a Blind Leap into the Dark

Some maintain that faith is a blind leap into the dark. The blinder the leap, the greater the faith. Have you ever heard this? In the 1989 film *Indiana Jones and the Last Crusade*, this mentality was put on the big screen. Indiana Jones was making his way through the caves through tests and trials as he attempted to retrieve the Holy Grail, which would bring life back to his dying father. The last test was a test of faith. Jones came upon a great chasm that separated him from the grail. But when he looked, there was no way across the chasm. The solution? A step of faith. After much hesitation, he closed his eyes, held his breath, and took the blind leap. His faith was rewarded as a bridge, unseen to the naked eye, suddenly appeared.

Take something as simple as a chair. God is the chair. He is asking you to sit down (rest) in the chair. If faith were a blind leap into the dark, this is what it might look like:

Fig. 5.1 Faith as a Blind Leap into the Dark

2. Faith as an Irrational Leap

For some, faith is something we have in spite of the evidence. While everything may militate against our faith, we make the most irrational choice of all. The more irrational the faith, the greater the faith. Here is what it looks like with the chair (notice that all the rationality is behind you).

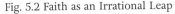

Fig. 5.2 Faith as an Irrational Leap

3. Faith as a Step according to the Evidence

The next option is that faith is a step according to rational evidence and inquiry. In other words, we believe because it makes sense. Everything in life, according to this view, takes faith. Even getting in your car and driving to work takes faith. You have to have faith that your car's brakes won't go out, that other drivers will not cross the yellow line, and that you won't fall asleep at the wheel. These are all steps of faith, but they don't need to be irrational or blind steps. We can have warranted trust in ourselves, other drivers, and our car due to our knowledge of these things. This is called "warranted faith." We make our decisions precisely because the evidence supports it, but this is still faith. This is what it might look like:

Fig. 5.3 Faith as a Step according to the Evidence

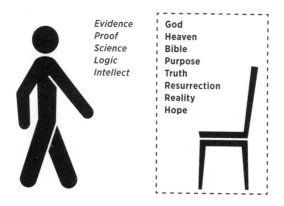

4. True Biblical Faith

It might surprise you to learn that while all of these are legitimate ways the word *faith* is used today, none of them represent the faith expressed in the Bible. The faith that God calls us to have is neither blind nor irrational. And while we believe our faith is the most rational choice that we can make given the evidence, rationale alone is not enough. The Bible says that without outside intervention, we are antagonistic to spiritual truths. If we rely on naked intellect or personal effort alone, even as Christians, we will never truly be able to rest in God.

The most important component to our faith has yet to be revealed. What is this element? It is the power of the Holy Spirit. The third member of the Trinity must ignite our faith. Yes, he uses rationale, inquiry, evidences, personal effort, and our minds to do so. But these things alone can get us only so far. In order to have true faith, the power of the Holy Spirit must move within us. True biblical faith looks like this:

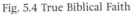

Fig. 5.4 True Biblical Faith

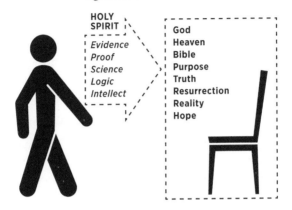

It is our will that is the problem. We don't have the will to trust in God alone. Consider what Paul says to the Corinthians:

> Now we have received not the spirit of the world, but the Spirit who is from God, that we might understand the things freely given us by God. And we impart this in words not taught by human wisdom but taught by the Spirit, interpreting spiritual truths to those who are spiritual. The natural person does not accept the things of the Spirit of God, for they are folly to him, and he is not able to understand them because they are spiritually discerned. (1 Cor. 2:12–14)

Any time we rely on ourselves to rest in God, we are acting as "natural" people. We have to act as spiritual people and call on God to increase our faith through the power of the Spirit as the Spirit energizes our will and intellect.

FAITH ALONE

While all three great Christian traditions (Catholicism, Eastern Orthodoxy, and Protestantism) believe that faith is absolutely necessary to be saved, Protestants uniquely emphasize that it is faith and *only* faith that justifies us (makes us right with God). It is always a temptation in our Christian walk to think that we somehow have earned the right to be a child of God. We will often try to build a résumé that is filled with all the great things we have done. We can begin to think that our salvation is based or dependent on our works. Whether it is going to church, giving money to the poor, or saying something nice about someone, we think that God loves us more because of the things we do. But the Bible says that it is our faith alone that brings us into God's family. And once there, we are loved no matter what.

In the sixteenth century, there was quite a battle in the church over this issue. To control and protect the gospel, the institutional church of the day began to set up all kinds of hurdles that Christians had to jump in order to maintain their relationship with God. The requirements were heavy. If you missed church, your salvation was in jeopardy. If you committed adultery, your relationship with God was severed. If you were excommunicated from the church, you were excommunicated from God. Because of this, people began to lose their confidence in God's love and their salvation.

Martin Luther, an Augustinian monk, came on the scene and was used by God to change things in a dramatic way. After years of guilt, fear, and self-flagellation, Luther, through studying the Bible, came to the conclusion that the institutionalized church was getting in the way. He realized that the Bible teaches that it is our faith alone, not good works, that are required. He realized that God's righteousness is not something that we have to live up to, but something we have to receive through faith by God's grace (unmerited gift) alone. Ephesians 2:8–9 says, "For by grace you have been saved through faith. And this is not your own doing; it is the gift of God, not a result of works, so that no one may boast." Luther's realization changed the landscape of the church through the rediscovery of the doctrine of justification. We call this change "The Great Reformation." As a result of the Reformation, men and women were liberated from ignorance once again as they realized that their relationship with God was not mediated by any church, pope, pastor, or institution, but through their faith in Christ alone.

Your standing before God is secure in your faith in Christ. Indeed, you will do great and wonderful things for God through your faith, but the things you do are not the instigator of your relationship with God, but rather the result of your faith. So it would be good right now to get some biblical mathematics down:

Good works $\neq$ justification
Faith + good works $\neq$ justification
Faith = justification + good works

THE THREE ASPECTS OF FAITH

With such an emphasis on faith, the Reformers, such as Martin Luther, sought to distinguish true faith from false faith. The battle cry of the Reformation, *sola fide* (justification *by faith alone*), demanded that they define faith in a precise manner.

Starting with Luther and further developed by Philipp Melanchthon, Francis Turretin, and others, the understanding of faith was expressed in three separate yet vitally connected aspects: *notitia*, *assensus*, and *fiducia*. (Hang with me as we learn some Latin terminology!) These are the three aspects of faith the Reformers said were necessary to have true faith.

1. *Notitia*. This is the basic informational foundation of our faith. It is best expressed by the word *content*. Faith, according to the Reformers, must have substance. In other words, you cannot have faith in nothing! There must be some referential propositional truth to which the faith points. For example, among other things, the propositions "God exists," "Christ rose from the grave," and "God loves us" form the information base that all Christians must have.

2. *Assensus*. This is the assent or *conviction* we have that the content is really true. We "assent" to the information. This involves evidence that leads to the conviction of the truthfulness of the said proposition. According to the Reformers, to have knowledge of the proposition is not enough. We must, to some degree, be convicted that it is indeed true. This involves intellectual assent and persuasion based upon critical thought. While *notitia* claims "Christ rose from the grave," *assensus* takes the next step and says, "I am persuaded to believe that Christ rose from the grave."

But these two alone are not enough, according to the Reformers. As one person has said, these two only qualify you to be a demon, for the demons both have the right information (Jesus rose from the grave) and are convicted of its truthfulness. One aspect still remains.

3. *Fiducia*: This is the "resting" in the information based upon a conviction of its truthfulness. *Fiducia* is best expressed by the English word "trust." If we are sticking with our C's, then we could use the word *consent*. We have the content, we are convicted of its truthfulness, and we consent to it. To use

the chair illustration, we have information that the object is a chair (content) and we believe it will hold us up (conviction). The final act is to sit in it (consent). Christ died for our sins (*notitia*). I believe that Christ died for my sins (*notitia* + *assensus*). I place my trust in Christ to save me (*fiducia*). Fiducia is the personal subjective act of the will to take the final step.

It is important for you to continually develop all three aspects of faith in your Christian life. Biblical, theological, and philosophical studies are good ways to build content. Intellectually wrestling with the issues involved helps conviction. We also have a discipline in Christian theological studies called "apologetics," which does not apologize for the faith, but seeks to intellectually defend the faith. Get engaged in apologetics, and you will have opportunities to greatly increase your conviction. Consent is an act of the will. Do you remember that the Christian faith is impossible without the power of the Holy Spirit energizing your faith? This is where this is most evident. Acting out your faith by resting in God is a work that only the Holy Spirit can perform. But, from the human perspective, we are to act out our faith by trusting in what God has said. Content, conviction, and consent are essential for Christian faith to grow and be real.

DEALING WITH DOUBT

Belief is not black-and-white. In other words, it is not as if you either have it or you don't. There will be many times when you doubt your faith. This is not *necessarily* a bad thing. The Bible says, "Have mercy on those who doubt" (Jude 22). This includes you. You must have mercy on yourself. You have an imperfect faith. One day our faith will be perfect. One day we will believe without any doubt whatsoever. But right now, we believe, but we also doubt. A man cried out to Christ, "I believe; help my unbelief!" (Mark 9:24). If this is your cry to God right now or becomes so sometime later in life, don't be too alarmed. Join the crowd. We sometimes doubt God's love, our salvation, even the very existence of God. Why? Because we will remain imperfect until the second coming of Christ.

In order to overcome your doubt, you must do many things.

First, don't mistake doubt with unbelief. Doubt does not necessarily mean you don't believe.

Second, don't suppress your doubt and put it in a closet in the back of your mind. Deal with it.

Third, realize that some of the greatest people in the Bible doubted. Christ says that John the Baptist is the greatest man to ever be born (Luke 7:28). Yet, at the very end of John the Baptist's life, he doubted Christ (Luke 7:19)! Amazing.

Fourth, lean on the faith of others when you doubt. This is called fellowship. It is called community. It is the "body of Christ" that aids us in all our weaknesses. Don't be ashamed when the faith of others must encourage you because your faith is lacking (Rom. 1:11–12).

Fifth, identify the source of your doubt. Sometimes doubt is an intellectual thing. In such cases, you will need to engage in apologetics (remember, this is the theological discipline of defending the faith). What are you doubting? The existence of God? The resurrection of Christ? The goodness of God in light of the existence of evil? The exclusivity of the Christian faith? Whatever the intellectual battle is, many good resources are available. Dig into them. Sometimes doubt is an emotional thing. We get mad at God, and we doubt. We can't understand why he is silent, and we doubt. He fails to answer our prayers in the ways we want, and we doubt. He brings suffering into our lives (more on this later), and we doubt. Sometimes we are chemically depressed, and we doubt. If emotional doubt is your issue, you must realize that you are not alone. Church history has identified this as "the dark night of the soul" because such doubt is dark and depressing. Why does God allow us to go through such times? Your guess is as good as mine. But the fact is, he does.

Finally, live according to the faith you *do* have, not the faith you don't have. Oftentimes when you doubt or are mad at God, you will adjust your life and begin to live like an unbeliever. This will only intensify the doubt and cause you more trouble. During times of doubt, continue to attend church, don't stop praying, read your Bible, and keep working hard for the Lord.

Doubt is something we all have to learn to live with. I pray that this encouragement will keep you strong during these times.

In this chapter I have tried to define and defend the Christian definition of faith, as opposed to many other ways the concept is defined. My prayer is that your faith never becomes rote like your drive to work or the way you shave. My prayer is that your faith will be alive, effective, and growing until it is perfected when we see Christ face to face: "For now we see in a mirror dimly, but then face to face. Now I know in part; then I shall know fully, even as I have been fully known" (1 Cor. 13:12).

DISCUSSION QUESTIONS

1. Some people say that Christianity is based only on faith. What do you think they mean?
2. How should we correct people's misunderstandings of faith? Give illustrations you can use to help correct them.

3. Why do you think it is so hard for us to rely *completely* on Christ? Why do we so often attempt to add to the work of Christ through our own efforts?

4. In churches today, which element of faith do you believe is lacking the most: content, conviction, or trust?

5. In *your* life right now, what do you find lacking the most: content, conviction, or trust? What can you do to change that?

ADDITIONAL DISCIPLESHIP TRAINING

Faith Alone, R. C. Sproul

Introduction to Theology, part 1 of The Theology Program, Credo House Ministries

Love Your God with All Your Mind, J. P. Moreland

6

Prayer

I'm going to ask you to do an odd thing. I want you to talk more to a person you don't see than to all the people you do see, combined. It is called prayer. Prayer is an essential part of your Christian discipleship.

God wants you to talk to him. It is that simple. He created you for a relationship with him. He did not *need* a relationship, as if he lacked anything. He did not create us because he was bored and lonely and needed someone to cheer him up, tell him how great he is, or give him advice. But he does want you to talk to him, continually. Think about it this way. My oldest child's first words were "da, da, da." I interpreted that as "daddy." This was an amazing first step to what has become an incredible and wonderful relationship built on communicating. If Katelynn grew but never talked at all, we would have been discouraged. Or, even more discouraging, what if she talked to everyone but me? What if she never said, "Daddy, help me. I hurt my leg"? Or, "Daddy, I'm hungry"? Or "Daddy, I don't feel so well"? Or, most importantly, "Daddy, I love you"? When you don't talk to people you know and love, could it be said that you really don't have a relationship with them at all?

God did not create us because he needed to be in relationship with someone. God has been in a relationship for all eternity. This relationship is within the Trinity. God the Father, God the Son, and God the Holy Spirit all love each other at the deepest level. They are in communion with each other. They love their relationship. When God created man, he could have created him individualistically. He could have created him without any ability or desire to have relationships. He could have withheld the ability to talk to others. But he did not. He created us in his image (Gen. 1:26).

I often think about God, at creation, showing man all of the great things he had created. When I was young, I would get many presents from many people on Christmas morning. Most of them would be wrapped and under the tree. But when all the presents were unwrapped and the feeling of Christmas morning was waning, my family knew that there was one present left yet to be revealed for each of us. They were from my dad. Dad would wait until everything was over, then disappear to some mysterious place for a few minutes. But we all knew what was coming. Dad would come in with a load of unwrapped presents. And these were the big ones. These were the bicycles, the electronics, the mobile phones, and all those things that cost the most. Though he would not show it on his face, I knew how excited he was. My dad's presents trumped all the others.

I think of prayer—the fundamental component of our relationship with God—in the same way as my dad's Christmas gifts. God was so excited to share so many gifts at creation. But "the big one" was that we get to have communion with him. The big one was that we, unlike all the plants and animals, get to have a relationship with him like he has with the other members of the Trinity.

Prayer and communion with God is part of our spiritual DNA. We are created to have communion with God. Of course, many rebel against this. Many people pray to other gods. Many attempt to manipulate God in prayer. And many people don't pray at all. What a waste of such a wonderful gift.

Unfortunately, prayer is often thought of as a chore. Some might advise you, "As a disciple of Christ, you have to pray to him continually." But this would get you off on the wrong foot. It is not that you *have to* pray to God continually, it is that you *get to* pray to God continually! It is a gift you have been given, and it fulfills one of our greatest desires and needs.

What is prayer? We could put it very simply and say that prayer is merely talking to God. This is true. There is nothing complicated about it. On a TV show I recently watched, a family who never prayed together decided to pray before Thanksgiving dinner. The father stood up as everyone else timidly bowed their heads, closed their eyes, and put their hands together in a very odd way (which is never seen except in cliché expressions of prayer). The father said, "Um, [ahem] . . . hi. I mean, dear God. I hope you are okay with us talking to you. You have not heard much from us . . . [ahem] . . . Well, thanks for all our family and stuff. Okay, I guess that is it . . . [ahem] . . . Over and out. Or . . . [ahem] . . . amen." It was rather comical to watch, because talking to God can be so hard for us sometimes. We often don't know how to talk to him or what to say.

THE BASICS OF PRAYER

Even the disciples were somewhat confused about prayer. One of the great and candid questions that these guys asked Jesus was how to pray: "Now Jesus was praying in a certain place, and when he finished, one of his disciples said to him, 'Lord, teach us to pray, as John taught his disciples'" (Luke 11:1).

Christ responded with what has become known as "the Lord's Prayer." I think a better description would be "the Disciples' Prayer," because it is not a private prayer that Christ prayed while on the earth; it is Christ's instruction about how we are to pray. The first thing that you must know about this prayer is that Jesus did not intend for it to be the only prayer that you say every time you pray to God. It is not to be a rote prayer. In fact, if you use it as a rote prayer that you simply memorize and say over and over again, you will be misusing it. God does not want us to say rote, memorized prayers that require little thought and interaction. Christ spoke against such things: "And when you pray, do not heap up empty phrases as the Gentiles do, for they think that they will be heard for their many words" (Matt. 6:7).

This makes sense. After all, how would you like someone you loved to say the exact same thing to you every day? What if my son Will were to say the same thing to me every morning: "Dad, I love you. I will miss you while at school. I will pray that you have a good day and I will try not to be bad." This might be awesome to hear the first time, but if it were repeated day after day, I would begin to suspect that he does not really mean it. More than that, a relationship requires more dynamics.

When Christ gave "the Disciples' Prayer," he intended it to be a *model* prayer that contains many (not all) of the essential elements of what God would love to hear from you. Here is the prayer in full:

Pray then like this:

> Our Father in heaven,
> hallowed be your name.

> Your kingdom come,
> your will be done,
>> on earth as it is in heaven.
> Give us this day our daily bread,
> and forgive us our debts,
>> as we also have forgiven our debtors.
> And lead us not into temptation,
>> but deliver us from evil. (Matt. 6:9–13)

Let's take some time to break this prayer down.

1. Prayer as Worship

"Our Father in heaven, hallowed be your name" (v. 9).

We recognize who God is and his relation to the universe. While God is our friend, he is also the eternal Creator of the universe who holds the fabric of time together. While prayer can be very casual, we need to be careful that we begin by recognizing who we are talking to. He is our Father "in heaven."

Next we have a sort of request: "Hallowed be your name." *Hallowed* means "holy" or "sanctified." It literally means, "Set apart" be your name. The "name" is not simply a handle of recognition, but an expression of God's entire being. It is his reputation, the way we are to think of him.

In the first part of this model prayer, we have a recognition of who we are talking to and an expressed desire to make sure we carry, discharge, and represent who he is with great accuracy and reverence. Translation: when you come to God in prayer make sure you know who you are talking to!

To *worship* is to give credence to the worth of something. When we worship God, we are recognizing who he is before all else. Therefore, we begin all prayer with proper worship.

2. Prayer as a Recognition of God's Will

"Your kingdom come, your will be done, on earth as it is in heaven" (v. 10).

Our prayers are to be submissive to God's will. In other words, we start by saying that what God wants is what we want. Ultimately, this is expressed by the coming of the kingdom. When I am out of town on a speaking engagement, the first thing my kids ask me over the phone is, "When are you coming home?" They have a great desire for me to be with them. I think this part of the model prayer is similar. When we pray, we are to have a great hope and expectation that God will be "home" soon.

"Your will be done, on earth as it is in heaven" expresses the understanding that when we come to God, we are looking for his plan to be accomplished, not ours. God is not a vending machine. He is not the great Granddad in heaven who simply wants to give us what we want. He is a Father who has a plan that is perfect. His plan (will) is what we are looking for. This does not mean we cannot ask God for things. It means that when we ask, we ask according to his will. We want his will, not ours, to be accomplished on earth, just as it is in heaven. This part of our prayer life takes great discipline and maturity. You will continually find yourself before God seeking only your will if you don't have this attitude of heart when you pray. And you'll find it a frustrating way to live with God.

3. Prayer as an Expression of Dependence

"Give us this day our daily bread" (v. 11).

This interesting phase is hard to understand in English. In fact, the Greek term we translate as "daily bread" is found only in this passage. Some early church fathers believed that this word was coined by the Gospel writers. "Daily bread" is a good translation, but verse 11 is about much more than a loaf of eatable substance. This part of our prayer expresses the complete dependence we must have on God. It is as if you are coming to God and leaning all your weight into his arms, recognizing that he is the only One who holds your life together. In your prayers, express this reliance: "God, my life, my purpose, my health, my family, and my protection are completely in your hands. Please provide for all my needs."

The idea of "daily" is important as well. Our lives are filled with many troubles *this very day*. Jesus says as much: "Therefore do not be anxious about tomorrow, for tomorrow will be anxious for itself. Sufficient for the day is its own trouble" (Matt. 6:34).

God wants you to focus on *today*, even in your prayer life. This does not mean that we don't plan for the future or even pray about things beyond today; it means that God wants us to put our lives in his hands *right now*! This part of the model prayer gives you permission—indeed, a mandate—to tell God everything you need even though he already knows it (Ps. 139:4).

4. Prayer as Confession

"Forgive us our debts, as we also have forgiven our debtors" (v. 12).

Here Jesus shows us the importance of transparency in prayer. God knows you inside and out. He knows everything you have done and everything you will ever do. He knows about your struggles, problems, and sinful habits. The point is that God wants you to be honest with him about your sins. Asking for forgiveness is one of the hardest things for humans to do. Our will fights against it with God and with others. We justify our wrongdoings in a thousand different ways. We hide them if we are able, and we defend them when we are not. God simply wants us to admit what he already knows and ask for forgiveness.

This does not mean that we are not already forgiven. The moment you trust in Christ, from a divine legal standpoint, all of your sins are taken care of. You cannot ever exist in a state of condemnation before God (Rom. 8:1). However, just because we cannot lose our legal standing before God, this does not mean that we cannot have relational problems with God as we try to hide our sins.

Consider this from the Gospel of John:

> Then he [Jesus] poured water into a basin and began to wash the disciples' feet and to wipe them with the towel that was wrapped around him. He came to Simon Peter, who said to him, "Lord, do you wash my feet?" Jesus answered him, "What I am doing you do not understand now, but afterward you will understand." Peter said to him, "You shall never wash my feet." Jesus answered him, "If I do not wash you, you have no share with me." Simon Peter said to him, "Lord, not my feet only but also my hands and my head!" Jesus said to him, "The one who has bathed does not need to wash, except for his feet, but is completely clean. And you are clean, but not every one of you." (John 13:5–10)

You are completely clean. Your sins have been forgiven. Yet you need your feet washed daily so that you can walk with God in fellowship. You need to "clear the air" before God. Recognizing your sins, as best you can, is an essential step in your prayer life.

5. Prayer as Deliverance in Warfare

"And lead us not into temptation, but deliver us from evil" (v. 13).

When Christ says, "Deliver us from evil," the text literally reads, "Deliver us from *the* evil." What is *the* evil? Many interpreters (including me) believe that it is Satan. In our Christian walks it can be easy to forget that we are in a *spiritual* battle. I forget this all the time. I have to remind myself that we are at war. Great news, eh? The moment you trusted in Christ is the moment you entered into a cosmic battle against invisible forces of evil. We need deliverance from this evil. Prayer is our defense against Satan.

Though Satan is a created being just like the rest of us, and though God could extinguish his life and purpose with a snap of a finger, God still lets him roam the earth, seeking to devour people (1 Pet. 5:8). Satan can only be in one place at one time, but there are many other dark forces who are on his side. We call them demons. They will attempt to influence and tempt you to sin, to fall away, to deny Christ, and to be weak in faith. We don't know why God lets them do what they do. We just know that he does. One day they will be judged, but for now they are invisible forces of evil who are allowed to oppress us if they can.

Every day we must recognize this battle and pray for God's protection. Ultimately, this is a prayer against temptation. We don't want to be tempted by evil. We should never have the attitude of arrogance. We can never say to temptations, "Bring it on." We need to run from temptation, knowing that we are weak. Charles Spurgeon, the great English Baptist preacher, used to pray, "When there is opportunity to sin, do not give me the desire. When there is desire to sin, do not give me the opportunity." This is a great prayer in our battle against evil.

We should continually pray that God would deliver us from temptation. You are not that strong. Pray that temptation does not come into your life.

ARGUING WITH GOD IN PRAYER

Most people hate arguments. I do. I especially hate arguments with my wife. But I am going to encourage you to argue with God. No, I don't mean an antagonistic venture where the emotions are fierce and the tension is high. What I mean is that I want you to present your case to God about things. Actually, it is God who wants you to make your case. An argument here means that you come to God, express your desire, and explain why you think he should respond according to your desires.

There are some great arguments with God in the Scriptures. When God is about to destroy Israel and reinvent his covenant purpose through Moses, Moses, out of concern for Israel, makes an argument for why God should not destroy his people (Ex. 32:11–14). We see Abraham present an argument to the Lord to spare Sodom in Genesis 18:23–32. And we see a rather odd encounter that Jacob has with God where he gets into an actual physical wrestling match with him (Gen. 32:22–32). I don't claim to understand the mystery of this battle, but it seems to represent the arguments that we have with God, which involve making our case for our requests.

Obviously with Moses, Abraham, and Jacob, God did not need outside wisdom to make the right decision. He knew exactly what he was going to do. It is the same with us. Can we change the mind of God through a well-reasoned argument? Yes and no. We can never alter God's true intentions. But our arguments are often the means by which God accomplishes his purpose.

The point is simple: God wants you to be so engaged in your prayer life that you are able to make an argument for your requests. It is as if God is asking you why, when you present your requests to him. "Why do you want me to heal you?" "Why do you want to get this job?" "Why do you want another child?" A well-reasoned argument does not guarantee that you will move the hand of God, but God does love you and he wants you to be so engaged with him that you can actually make a case for your requests.

THE LOGISTICS OF PRAYER

Let me briefly speak about the logistics of prayer. First, you should know that there is no "right" way to pray. People are seen in the Bible as praying on their knees (1 Kings 18:42), standing up (Neh. 9:3–5), sitting down (Luke 24:30), with eyes open (John 11:41), and with their faces on the ground (2 Chron. 7:3). God does not care so much about the place you pray or the position in which you pray. He hears you from wherever you are (Ps. 139:7–10). What God cares about is your heart. He is glad to hear from you wherever you are and however you look.

In Jesus's Name

You have probably heard the phrase "in Jesus's name" on the lips of many Christians as they conclude a prayer. For many of us, this phrase is so ingrained in us that we can say it without thinking about what it really means. Not long ago my sister called me on the phone and left a message. At the end of the message, instead of saying the normal "good-bye," she accidently said, "In Jesus's name, amen." This mistake has been the fodder for many laughs in my family. But it shows how we can use this phrase in a habitual and meaningless way.

Indeed, Christ did encourage us to ask for things in his name (John 14:13–14). But this phrase is not some magic formula that guarantees the prayer will be answered. It demonstrates recognition of our standing. To pray "in Jesus's name" is what we are doing, whether we know it or not. As Christians, our only audience with the Father is through the Son. When you trusted Christ, you were clothed in his righteousness. When God sees you, he sees you as he sees Christ—perfect. Therefore, we are "in Jesus's name" in the sense that we are standing in the circle of grace that he created for us. We come to God in the name of Jesus. What a great standing to have!

To Whom Do We Pray?

Do we pray to the Father, Son, or Holy Spirit? Most Christians for the last two thousand years have directed their prayers to the Father. This seems legitimate, as the model prayer starts with "Our Father." However, some passages of Scripture show prayer directed to Jesus (John 14:14; Rom. 10:13; Acts 7:59; Rev. 22:20). While we don't have any examples of prayers directed to the Holy Spirit, there is nothing wrong with praying to him, as well.

So, to whom do we pray? While it is fine for you to pray to any of the members of the Trinity, or just "God" in general, the great traditions of Christian thought encourage us to pray to the Father, through the Son, and by the Spirit.

God wants us to talk to him. It may seem odd talking to someone you don't see, but you are not crazy for doing so. The God of all eternity loves you and wants to hear from you all the time. In fact, Scripture commands us to "pray without ceasing" (1 Thess. 5:17). I pray that you never see prayer as a burden that you have to fit it on your calendar. Prayer is a gift. Prayer is an opportunity. Prayer is an essential component to your walk with God. It is a present that God has given us. It is as if he says to us, "Guess what? I want to have a relationship with you. I am listening to you *all* the time. I hear every word you say and every thought you think. I can't wait to hear from you!"

DISCUSSION QUESTIONS

1. Why do you think the God of the universe desires to be in constant communication with us?
2. Why do you think it is important for us to prioritize our need for "today"?
3. We are to pray against the forces of Satan. Why do you think God allows Satan to tempt us?
4. Why do you think God may want us to make an argument for the things we request of him?
5. In what ways do we often get too busy to pray? How can you prevent this in your life?

ADDITIONAL DISCIPLESHIP TRAINING

Lord, Teach Us to Pray, Andrew Murray

Prayer, Philip Yancey

The Pursuit of God, A.W. Tozer

7

Study

Christians believe the Bible is the Word of God. We believe that it is *inspired*. We believe that it is a book like no other. It was written completely by God and completely by man. Confused? Join the crowd! While prayer describes our talking to God, Bible study describes his communication to us. But the Bible can be hard to understand. Often, interpreters can't agree on what many passages mean. This is part of the reason why the Bible is the most controversial book ever written. It has divided countries and families. It creates divisions, splits churches, and can be downright frustrating to read. The Bible study method we are going to focus on will not guarantee that you always understand the Bible perfectly, but it will guarantee that you are interpreting the Bible with integrity before God and having a legitimate interaction with God.

COMMON BIBLE STUDY METHODS

First, let's look at eight common Bible study methods that can steer you toward the *wrong* path.

1. Lucky Lotto

(Eyes closed): "Umm . . . I will read *this* verse."

Oftentimes, you may be tempted to simply ask God a question, open up the Bible, fix your eyes on the first verse you see, and think that you've found God's answer. There is an old story of a depressed man who did this. He opened up his Bible to Matthew 27:5: "He went and hanged himself." A bit confused, the man did it again. This time his eyes fell on John 13:27: "What you are going to do, do quickly." Now, that was not lucky at all.

We must understand that the Bible, while inspired, is not a magic book. God does not speak through it out of context. Every passage has a message that needs to be understood within a context. Be careful not to practice "lucky lotto" Bible studies.

2. Brussels Sprout

"Do I have to?"

Many people hate to study the Bible like they hate to eat their vegetables. You must find a way to cultivate a love for sitting at the feet of God through Bible study. I know just as well as anyone that Bible study can be long and laborious, especially when you are in certain books that don't seem to produce much fruit from your labor. But always remember that you have the opportunity *to hear from the God of all eternity*. Bible study is a privilege. When it becomes a burden, think through your life and your commitment to God. For me, Bible study is more of a burden on days that I am not so fully committed to him. But when my life is on track, Bible study is often the best part of my day.

3. Channel Changer

"Let's read something else."

It is easy to jump from place to place every time you study

your Bible. But try to be disciplined to stick to one book at a time. Think about it in relation to movies. We don't watch bits and pieces of dozens of different movies. We start a movie at the beginning, and we don't stop until it is over. This is the way I want you to approach the Bible. Work your way through entire books, becoming completely immersed in what each one has to teach, then move on to the next. It is OK to read many books at a time, but make sure that you are not always jumping around, thereby never getting the whole story.

4. The Concorde

"Watch how fast I can finish."

When I was a kid, I used to feel so guilty about not reading the Bible. My mother taught me about the importance of Bible study, and I kept a Bible beside my bed wherever I went. But it was hard for me to actually read my Bible. I don't know why. When I did guilt myself into reading it, I would always pick the shortest chapter I could find (usually in the Psalms) and blow through it at lightning speed. I wonder what God thought of that. "OK, God, I am ready to listen. Just talk as fast as you can and let's get this over with." I doubt he honored me with much insight. The point is to *put on the brakes*. Read your Bible slowly. Read your Bible carefully. Pray before, during, and after you read. Talk to God while you are reading. Talk out loud if you have to. This will make you much more engaged, and it will produce much more fruit in your study.

5. Baseball Card

"I'm very picky."

Some people like certain parts of the Bible more than others. In my Bible, the pages of the Upper Room Discourse in

John 14–17 are more worn than any other section. This is because Jesus's words, "Let not your hearts be troubled" (14:1, 27) are so comforting! I find certain parts of the Bible more challenging than others. For example, the Law can be archaic and boring. The Prophets can be hard to understand. However, I must discipline myself to be intimately acquainted with the entire Bible. Yes, some things will seem more relevant than others, but God wants us to know the *whole* story, not just the parts we like. I encourage you to try to go through the entire Bible every year (there are some great Bible reading plans you can easily access). You can continue to read those passages you love over and over. But make sure you are getting the whole picture.

6. Clint Eastwood

"I don't need anyone's help."

We all need help. Bible study is wonderful, but it is tough. Make sure you lean on many of the great people today and from throughout church history to aid you in your studies. Yes, you have the Holy Spirit in you, and you can understand much. But the Holy Spirit works primarily through the community called the body of Christ. This is true in Bible study as well. Many Bible study aids are available, but the best works are called *commentaries*. These are books written by people who have spent their whole lives studying the Bible. Once you determine to read a particular book of the Bible, find a good commentary to help you through the difficulties that are sure to arise.

7. Magical

"Abracadabra—it applies to my life."

Some people call the Bible "God's Love Letter to You." We have to be careful with this kind of sentiment. The Bible was not really written to *you*. The Bible was written to people who lived thousands of years ago, were in a completely different culture, and had very specific needs and problems. Rightly understood, the Bible will often have principles that apply to your life, but these principles must be gleaned by interpreting the Bible through the lens of time. This is why it is important to understand the context of each and every passage and story. Sometimes it will have direct application to your life, but sometimes it is just God telling you about what happened, with no encouragement to follow the examples.

8. Indiana Jones

"Let's find the hidden meaning."

The Indiana Jones approach to Bible study assumes that there is some hidden meaning in Scripture that we must mine out. This is a dangerous approach. It assumes that we have some sort of secret decoder ring to find layers of truth hidden by God and discernible only to the Christian. But God did not write the Bible with the intent to have secret truth discernible only by a select few. He wrote it to reveal truth to all who will listen! There are no hidden messages in the Bible. Applying the proper study methods I describe below will guard you against this often divisive and subjective approach.

THREE STEPS TO STUDYING THE BIBLE

The Bible is two thousand years old and can seem archaic. Sometimes it is hard to know how it applies to us. The following is a practical guide to biblical interpretation. It follows a three-step process that I have used for years. This process has served me well, and I believe it is representative of the best way to interpret the ancient Word of God and apply it to today.

I hope that it will alleviate some of the "Bible interpretation anxiety" that you might have, allowing the Bible to become real and relevant to your life.

We are going to get technical, so put your thinking cap on.

Fig. 7.1 Three Steps to Studying the Bible

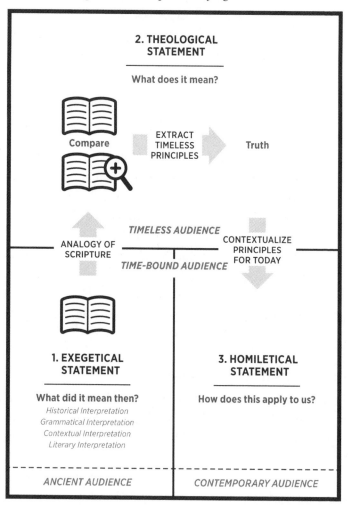

Notice the three sections of figure 7.1. There are three audiences that everyone needs to recognize in the process of interpreting the Bible. In the bottom left, we have the "ancient audience." This represents the original audience and the original author. The top portion represents the "timeless audience," which transcends the time and the culture of the original situation. Here we would put that which applies to all people of all places of all times, without regard to cultural and historical issues. Finally, we have the "contemporary audience" in the bottom right. This is the audience of today. Here we will find application of the Bible with regard to our time, culture, and circumstances.

In biblical interpretation, it is important that you go in the order of the chart. The goal is to find out what the Bible *meant*, what it *means*, and how it *applies* to us. Get that down: (1) meant, (2) means, (3) applies. Many people start with the third step and fail miserably in understanding God's Word. Others start with step two, attempting to force their own beliefs on the text. It is important that all steps are covered to ensure interpretive fidelity.

Step 1: Exegetical Statement: "What Did It Mean Then?"

The first step is the most important. Here, the goal is to ascertain the original intent of the writing. It is important that one enters into the world of the author and the audience. Sometimes this will be easy, but sometimes it will be difficult, requiring quite a lot of study. This search for meaning in the Bible is called *exegesis*, which means "to lead out." We want to bring out what is in the Bible, not read into it what we think it should say.

Here are the different issues we must consider.

Historical issues. Historical circumstances can aid in your understanding of the text. You will ask questions of "occasion." Who was the original author? Who was the original audience? What purpose did the writing have? For example, when Moses wrote the Pentateuch (the first five books of the Bible), what was his occasion or purpose? Was it to give an exhaustive history of the world to everyone, or to prepare the Israelite religious community to exist in a theocratic society under Yahweh? When Paul wrote his letter to the Corinthians, what was his purpose? Knowing that in 2 Corinthians he wrote to defend his apostleship as other false apostles were opposing him is essential to understanding every verse. What was Paul's disposition toward the Galatians when he wrote to them? Was it to commend, condemn, or correct? The occasion will determine much of our understanding. Ask these questions of each and every book you read in the Bible.

Grammatical issues. It is important to understand that the Bible was written in a different language. The New Testament was written in Greek. Not only that, but it was a particular kind of Greek called "Koiné." Most of the Old Testament was written in Hebrew (small portions were written in Aramaic). Naturally, other languages will have characteristics that communicate well in the original tongue but can get lost in translation. Greek, for example, works off inflections (word endings), which determine a word's part of speech. Word placement can add emphasis. These types of things are often hard to translate. I am not saying that everyone needs to be a Greek and a Hebrew scholar to understand the Bible. But there are grammatical issues that can nuance our understanding of the passage. A good commentary will point these out.

Contextual issues. Every book of the Bible was written for a purpose. The smallest component of a writing is a letter. We don't take each letter in isolation, however, but we understand that a group of letters makes a word. But we don't read words in isolation. We understand that a group of words makes a sentence. And we don't understand sentences in isolation. We understand that a group of sentences makes a paragraph. But we don't stop there. Each paragraph either represents or is a part of a larger whole that we call a *pericope*. The pericope is the basic argument or story that is being told. The story of David and Goliath is a pericope of many paragraphs. Christ's parables make up individual pericopes. Finally, the pericopes are smaller parts of an entire book. The purpose of the book will shape the context in which each pericope should be interpreted.

Figure 7.2 demonstrates how it looks:

Fig. 7.2 Discovering the Context

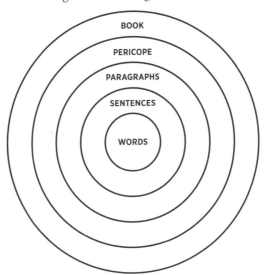

Literary issues. We must remember that there is no type of literature called "Bible" or "Scripture." The Bible is made up of many books from many different types of literature called *genres.* When you encounter different types of literature, you almost instinctively know that they follow different rules of understanding. In everyday life, you might come across novels, newspaper editorials, commercials, television dramas, academic textbooks, and tickers at the bottom of news stations. All of these need to be understood and interpreted according to the rules of the genre. The Bible contains narratives, histories, parables, apocalyptic prophecies, personal letters, public letters, songs, proverbs, and many others. Each of these is to be interpreted according to the rules of the genre. Just because they are in the Bible does not mean that the rules change. For example, a proverb is a common type of literature found in the Bible, but it is also found in many other cultures. A proverb is a statement of general truth or wisdom that does not necessarily apply in every situation. A proverb is not a promise. If it is in the Bible, it is *still* not a promise. Similarly, theological histories are just that—theological. That they are in the Bible does not turn them into a technically precise and exhaustive histories that answer every question we have. We must determine the type of literature we are dealing with if we are to understand it. Figure 7.3 should help us understand the genres of the Bible.

Fig. 7.3 Genres of the Bible

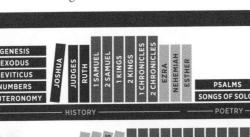

Step 2: Theological Statement:
"What Does It Mean for All People of All Places of All Times?"

Here is where we move from what *was* being said to what *is always* being said; from what *was* being taught to what *is always* being taught; and from what the original human author *was* saying to his audience to what God the Author *is always* saying to all people. The audience here is timeless and universal. We extract timeless principles for all people, of all places, of all times.

A principle is a timeless truth, a doctrine, a fundamental law. It is the underlying reality, the essence of an action, and the reason for the norm.

Sometimes it is easy to identify the principle of a passage of Scripture, especially when there is no cultural baggage to extract or interpret. Other times, finding the principle can be difficult. And sometimes a passage contains no universal principles. It's important to remember that more often than not, the text will only be communicating what was done, without any mandate to follow the example. For example, when we read that Paul told Timothy to bring him his cloak he had left in Troas (2 Tim. 4:13), we are not to universalize this particular verse to mean that Christians are supposed to bring people coats, clothes, or anything else to warm themselves. We must distinguish between what is *prescribed* and what is merely *described*.

Prescribed: a principle of truth telling us what to do.

Described: something that we are told about, but not necessarily encouraged to do.

Some material in the Bible is already in its principled (prescribed) form. For example, the author of Hebrews says that Jesus Christ said, "I will never leave you nor forsake you" (Heb. 13:5). In the context, this is a principle. We have no reason to think that Jesus is saying this only to the recipients of the book in the first century, but we have every reason to believe that this applies to all Christians of all times.

One way to determine whether something is a principle is to follow what we call the "analogy of Scripture" (see Fig. 7.1). We must ask whether passages elsewhere in the Bible confirm, repeal, or deny the principle or action in question. For example, much of the Law in the Old Testament does not apply to us today, theologically or in practice. Why? Because Christ fulfilled the law. The New Testament explicitly tells us that we are not under the law. Therefore, for example, we no longer offer animal sacrifices. Christ's sacrifice fulfilled this law. On the other hand, the command to not commit adultery is never repealed, and it is in fact confirmed and affirmed throughout Scripture. "You shall not commit adultery" is a universal principle.

Once a solid interpretation has been made, we can look for reinforcement of the principle from outside of Scripture. These interpretive aids should never be thought of as more authoritative than Scripture itself, but they can help us come to sound conclusions. Let's look again at four such aids (which we first examined in chap. 1):

1. *Reason.* Is the interpretation reasonable? Does it make sense? I am not talking here in a subjective sense, but in a very formal sense. If your interpretation directly conflicts with other known information, then the filter of reason will drive you back to Scripture to reassess your conclusion. Truth cannot contradict itself. The filter of reason will provide a valuable avenue of assessment concerning your interpretation.

2. *Tradition.* What do others say about it? Dipping into the well of the interpretive community can be extremely helpful. We believe that the Holy Spirit is in all Christians. Therefore, we can expect to find aid from the advice of the Spirit-led community. We are to look not only to contemporary scholars and theologians, but also to church history. What has the church said about a particular passage or issue throughout time? If you come to a different conclusion than the historic

body of Christ, it is a good sign that you have taken a wrong interpretive turn somewhere (though this might not always be the case).

3. *Experience*. Albeit fallible, our experience is an important interpretive guide. If your interpretation militates against your experience, it *could* be a sign that your interpretation is wrong. For example, after reading what Christ says in the Upper Room Discourse, "Whatever you ask in my name, this I will do" (John 14:13), we could get the idea that we can ask for *anything* in his name and expect to receive it. "Please give me a million bucks, in Jesus's name." "Please heal my mother, in Jesus's name." "Please remove this depression, in Jesus's name." I have been there and done that. We all have. When the magic formula does not work in our experience, we return to Scripture to search for other interpretive options. God expects and requires the use of experience in our interpretation of Scripture. The Bible is impossible to understand without an assumption of experience. While experience can lead us wrong, it can also help us to figure out how to rightly interpret Scripture.

4. *Emotion*. Our emotions can be extremely important, and but they can also be extremely misleading. First, they are important by analogy. In order for us to understand what the Bible says about God's love, we are expected to have had some degree of the emotion ourselves. For us to know what "the peace of God, which surpasses all understanding" in Philippians 4:7 is, we must have experienced some sort of peace in our lives. Otherwise, our understanding would be limited. Second, our emotions can direct us to the right understanding. We are told that the Holy Spirit convicts us of the truth (John 16:8). This internal conviction must be a valid source of information. If we feel that an interpretation of a passage is wrong because

it does not seem to be emotionally satisfying, this *could* be an indication that it is indeed wrong. But we must be careful, because our emotions are guided by many other sinful elements that can lead us to wrong interpretations. Nevertheless, part of the interpretive process is recognizing the role our emotions play in our understanding of Scripture. If we deny them and act as if they have no part to play, we are only fooling ourselves.

Extraction of the Principles

Once your interpretation has been filtered through the four interpretive aids, cultural baggage must be identified and extracted. Again, this involves separating the principles from the way in which these principles are applied in various contexts. Skipping this step is tremendously dangerous. Failing to realize that cultural issues have often determined the application of a principle can make the Bible seem irrelevant. Some cultural *expressions* are not timeless. For example, Paul tells the Romans to "greet one another with a holy kiss" (Rom. 16:16). While the principle of showing affection is timeless, if you don't extract that principle and apply it properly in your context, you might find yourself in a heap of trouble as you attempt to kiss someone you should not be kissing. In other words, the act of greeting people with a kiss will not be an acceptable way of showing affection in some cultures.

We find another such example in 1 Corinthians 11. Paul speaks to the Corinthian church about the necessity of women's head coverings. We must ask ourselves whether women wearing head coverings is an eternal requirement of God, or whether there is some underlying principle that it represents. Most of the women in my church do not wear hats or any sort of covering at all. Does this mean that they do not believe or submit to the Scriptures? Doing a historical study of this issue reveals that in the Corinthian culture (just as in many cultures today), head coverings probably represented both a woman's submission to her husband and her modesty. In that culture, a woman's hair was a representative and revelation of her beauty. Failing to wear a head covering was sexually provocative *in that culture*. It had implications toward marital bonds and fidelity. However, modesty and fidelity are the timeless principles, not simply the wearing of a hat. In this case, extracting the timeless principle means that the cultural baggage of expression—the head covering—gets discarded so that the real issue can come into focus.

We must do our best to distinguish that which is timebound from that which is timeless. Then, and only then, will we be prepared for step 3.

Step 3: Homiletical Statement: "How Does It Apply to Us?"

Having performed the first two steps, we now have all we need to contextualize the timeless principles for the twenty-first century.

Let's continue with the example of the head covering. Let's see if we can take the basic timeless principles and apply them to us. In twenty-first-century America, head coverings or hats have no relevance toward modesty or submission. So they don't communicate the same things that they did in first-century Corinth. Immodesty and lack of submission today might involve other things, such as short skirts and low-cut tops. Wearing these would break the principles of modesty and submission. You see, the principles still apply today, just in other ways.

Regarding the "holy kiss" in Romans 16, kissing someone in our culture communicates sexual intimacy, which was not Paul's idea. Paul just wanted people to show their affection for each other with an expression of kindness. In our culture, we do this through a handshake or a hug. These are both acceptable, and they fulfill the timeless principle of the passage.

Again, this applies only to the materials that have made it through the first two steps of the process intact. Historical details, incidentals, and descriptive material will never find *this type* of immediate and practical application. With much of Scripture, the primary application for us will be to *believe* it. I believe that God delivered the Israelites from bondage. It is a historical event that expresses God's faithfulness to his promises. Broadly speaking, I can use this as an illustration of God's faithfulness to his promises. But I cannot extract a timeless principle that says God will deliver all people from all their pain in this life, and then apply it to my immediate situation by saying God will deliver me from the difficulties I am going through. Only the timeless principles qualify for specific, present-day application.

I pray that this three-step process will be eternally valuable in your discipleship. Learning to listen to God is so important. Hearing him wrongly can be destructive to your Christian walk. Let me end this chapter with a hard illustration for me to share.

Many years ago, my sister was sick with depression. She had already tried to commit suicide once. This depression went on for over a year. My mother, a very godly woman, spent these days crying out to God to find an answer. I want to assure you that God has promised you a lot of things. But God has *not* promised a lot of things as well. Many times you will be tempted in your Christian walk to read into the Scriptures promises that he has never made. My mother became desperate, wanting my sister to be healed. She was scared and frustrated. Finally one day while reading the Bible and praying, my mom came upon a verse that she said "God gave her" about my sister. It was in the Psalms. She had a deep feeling that God was talking to her through this verse. She believed that God told her that my sister was going to be healed. My mother banked on this verse. The problem was that this verse said nothing about God promising to heal my sister. There was no precept or principle that even suggested such. But my mother, in emotional turmoil and desperation, forced this passage to fit her needs. My sister died a few months later. My mother blamed God. She thought God had failed her.

I want you to understand how important it is that you read and study your Bible. But I would rather you not read it than to read it and make the fundamental mistakes I have described in this chapter. This is why the Bible is a dangerous book. It is very powerful when interpreted correctly. But when it is interpreted wrongly, it can destroy people's lives, split churches, and bring about all kinds of troubles. If we properly interpret the Scriptures consistently, we will be less prone toward discouragement, disillusionment, and distancing ourselves from God. The Bible is rich and full of application and information, but it is not a magic book or a wax nose. It means what it means. Proper biblical interpretation through following the steps outlined above will serve us well.

DISCUSSION QUESTIONS

1. Of all the wrong ways to approach Bible study expressed at the beginning of this chapter, which do you have the tendency to drift into? Why?

2. We often think of the Bible as a magic book that automatically applies to our lives. Why do you think this is?
3. When is the best time for you to study your Bible? Why?
4. When you come to parts of Scripture that seem boring, what is some motivation for you to continue to study?
5. Why do you think God has chosen to communicate to us through a two-thousand-year-old book rather than just speaking directly to us?

ADDITIONAL DISCIPLESHIP TRAINING

Bibliology and Hermeneutics, part 2 of The Theology Program, Credo House Ministries

How to Read the Bible for All Its Worth, Gordon Fee and Douglas Stuart

Living by the Book, Howard and William Hendricks

8

Church

My three sisters and I fought like cats and dogs when we were kids (really, like three cats and one dog!). That is what siblings do when they are young. But now, my two living sisters are my best friends in the world. We lean on each other for support. We know each other better than just about anyone. When I have something to celebrate or mourn, I call my sisters first. We encourage and lift one another up. We would die for each other. Why? Because we are family. Of course, we still let each other down at times. We have very different personalities. We irritate each other. We hold different views about important issues. We even give each other the cold shoulder from time to time. But in the end, we are family. Forgiveness and reconciliation will always be found. And nothing can change this.

I am pleased to introduce you to your new family. When you trusted in Christ, you became a child of God and you inherited many new bothers and sisters. We often call them our bothers and sisters "in Christ." This means that you are spiritually related to many new people. Their numbers are in the millions, both alive and dead. And the reality is that, from

God's perspective, you are more related to this spiritual family than you are your own blood. Isn't that amazing?

WHAT IS THE CHURCH?

We call this new family the "church." Another way Christians put it is the "body of Christ." Why is it called the body of Christ? The idea here is that Christ is the head and we are the hands, feet, eyes, and ears. We are a family of believers who are Christ's activity here on earth. Christ has gone to heaven and will not come back until the time when all believers will be resurrected and all unbelievers will be judged. But in the meantime, we are Christ's body, the primary way in which he conducts his business here on earth.

The apostle Paul talks about this clearly in his first letter to the Corinthians:

> For in one Spirit we were all baptized into one body—Jews or Greeks, slaves or free—and all were made to drink of one Spirit.
>
> For the body does not consist of one member but of many. If the foot should say, "Because I am not a hand, I do not belong to the body," that would not make it any less a part of the body. And if the ear should say, "Because I am not an eye, I do not belong to the body," that would not make it any less a part of the body. If the whole body were an eye, where would be the sense of hearing? If the whole body were an ear, where would be the sense of smell? But as it is, God arranged the members in the body, each one of them, as he chose. If all were a single member, where would the body be? As it is, there are many parts, yet one body.
>
> The eye cannot say to the hand, "I have no need of you," nor again the head to the feet, "I have no need

of you." On the contrary, the parts of the body that seem to be weaker are indispensable, and on those parts of the body that we think less honorable we bestow the greater honor, and our unpresentable parts are treated with greater modesty, which our more presentable parts do not require. But God has so composed the body, giving greater honor to the part that lacked it, that there may be no division in the body, but that the members may have the same care for one another. If one member suffers, all suffer together; if one member is honored, all rejoice together.

Now you are the body of Christ and individually members of it. (1 Cor. 12:13–27)

We all have an important part to play in this body called the church. In other words, you have a job to do. You may be an eye, ear, foot, or pinky toe. No matter how God has gifted you, you are a part of the DNA of Christ—the church—and God has a job for you in this body.

VISIBLE AND INVISIBLE CHURCH

When most people hear the word *church*, they think of a building. They think of a structure that has chairs or pews facing a podium, an altar, maybe some stained-glass windows, and a nursery. Oh, and don't forget the steeple! But the church is not a building. The church is not even a pastor, pope, or choir. You don't have to have any of these things to have the church. The church is a body of people who have trusted in Christ. Even if you have never "gone to" church, you are a part of it.

We need to distinguish between the visible church and the invisible church. The visible church is made up of all those who are alive and *claim* to be followers of Christ. When you "go to" church, you enter into this visible body. The visible church is made up of Protestants, Roman Catholics, and Eastern Orthodox. It is represented by Baptists, Presbyterians, Lutherans, and house church Christians. It is fractured and divided. Sometimes these divisions are good and legitimate; sometimes they are very unfortunate. Here is what the visible church looks like:

Fig. 8.1 Major Christian Traditions

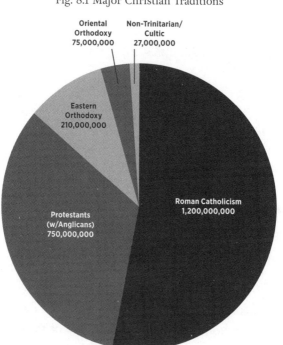

Fig. 8.2 Christian Denominations

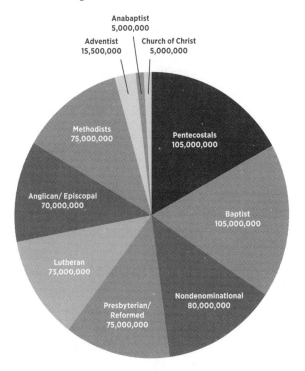

The visible church imperfectly represents Christ and is filled with true believers and false believers (Matt. 7:21–22).

The invisible church is the fellowship of true believers, both alive and dead. This includes all those who have truly trusted in Christ from every tradition or denomination. These believers may go to different visible churches, but they are all one family. You are part of the invisible church. No matter what your tradition or denomination, or lack thereof, you are in this family.

Yet, I am going to encourage you to be a part of the visible church. The saints of old used to call it *ecclesia militans*.

It means "the church militant." Isn't that great? The church militant is the body of true believers, within the church visible, here on earth battling sin, the flesh, and the Devil. That is you! You are in an army. The visible church attempts (and often fails) to express the invisible church. But its failure does not mean we ever give up the battle.

The body of Christ is a family and the body of Christ an army. I love it!

WHY DO WE NEED THIS FAMILY?

You need this family. This family needs you. You might think you don't *have* to be involved in this family. You might choose to never have a relationship with your siblings. You might be one of those people who, when wronged by a family member, never forgives. You might be someone who just does not have time for your family. But this does not please God, and it handicaps the church. You see, even if your function in the body of Christ is that of a pinky toe, you will be sorely missed, because you are needed for proper functioning of the body. Listen to what the book of Hebrews says: "And let us consider how to stir up one another to love and good works, not neglecting to meet together, as is the habit of some, but encouraging one another, and all the more as you see the Day drawing near" (Heb. 10:24–25). We are not to neglect getting together with other believers.

Figure 8.3 uses logs and fire to illustrate the importance of fellowship with other believers.

Fig. 8.3 The Importance of Fellowship with Other Believers

*Campfire designed by Megan Sheehan
from The Noun Project*

These are all the activities we take part in when we are with other believers. What happens to a log when it is alone? The fire goes out. What happens when it is placed with other logs? The fire roars! In the body of Christ, the fire can only roar when we are together exercising these activities. Let's examine each one briefly.

Fellowship

We sometimes call fellowship *koinonia*, a Greek word expressing community. According to Acts 2, the first New Testament church experienced this *koinonia*. Listen to what they did:

> So those who received his word were baptized, and there were added that day about three thousand souls.

And they devoted themselves to the apostles' teaching and the fellowship, to the breaking of bread and the prayers. And awe came upon every soul, and many wonders and signs were being done through the apostles. And all who believed were together and had all things in common. And they were selling their possessions and belongings and distributing the proceeds to all, as any had need. And day by day, attending the temple together and breaking bread in their homes, they received their food with glad and generous hearts, praising God and having favor with all the people. And the Lord added to their number day by day those who were being saved. (Act 2:41–47)

Isn't this great! The church acted like a family: sharing with each other, hanging out with each other, supporting each other, and eating together (which, in my opinion, is the best fellowship activity).

Ordinances

Christ commanded two primary activities as an expression of faith: baptism and the Lord's Supper.

Baptism is an outward expression of an inward change. The act of going down into water and coming up out of water illustrates what happened to us when we trusted in Christ. In Romans 6:1–7 Paul shows how in baptism it is as if we died with Christ, our old self was buried, and then our new self came to life with Christ. Baptism is an illustration of our spiritual birth into the family of God. It is important that you get baptized as soon as possible, if you have not already. You only do this once. Talk to your local church minister for more information.

The Lord's Supper is an ordinance that we should participate in on a regular basis. We pause with other believers and remember what Christ has done for us through the vivid illustration of eating bread (which represents his body) and drinking wine (which represents his blood). We partake of the Lord's Supper for two reasons: First, it should cause us to review our lives and fellowship with the Lord. Many in the Corinthian church were not taking this seriously:

> Whoever, therefore, eats the bread or drinks the cup of the Lord in an unworthy manner will be guilty concerning the body and blood of the Lord. Let a person examine himself, then, and so eat of the bread and drink of the cup. For anyone who eats and drinks without discerning the body eats and drinks judgment on himself. That is why many of you are weak and ill, and some have died. (1 Cor. 11:27–30)

The Corinthians were casually taking the Lord's Supper, without prayer or confession. It did not go well for them, so be careful that you take this seriously.

Second, the Lord's Supper proclaims and remembers Christ in a vivid way that expresses the deepest level of community, when done right. When you participate in the Lord's Supper with other believers (you cannot do it alone), you are all expressing to each other a covenant renewal with God. It is a beautiful picture of our shared belief in Christ's work on the cross.

Discipline

When we hear the word *discipline*, we normally think of parents punishing their children for disobedience. But discipline in the church is not quite like that. Discipline is an important part of our goal to become more Christlike. Matthew addresses the process of church discipline:

> If your brother sins against you, go and tell him his fault, between you and him alone. If he listens to you, you have gained your brother. But if he does not listen, take one or two others along with you, that every charge may be established by the evidence of two or three witnesses. If he refuses to listen to them, tell it to the church. And if he refuses to listen even to the church, let him be to you as a Gentile and a tax collector. (Matt. 18:15–17)

There is a proper way carry out discipline in the church. God intends it to restore relationships and shape souls. Only the most humble can accept church discipline without rebellion. Most of the time churches don't practice discipline for fear that the disciplined party will just leave the church and go somewhere else. This may at times happen, but I expect more from you. You must submit yourself to the collective wisdom of the body of Christ. It is very hard. Discipline involves submitting yourself to others. It can range from removing someone from the worship team due to a drug habit to calling a private meeting to discuss allegations of cheating on a business deal.

If you are having trouble with the idea of church discipline, think of its opposite. Think of a community of believers who claim to love their brothers and sisters but never say a word or do a thing when a brother is beating his wife. Think of a community that keeps its mouth shut when someone is killing himself with drugs. Could you really say that this is a community that cares?

Accountability

You are to make yourself accountable to others. You see, you still have a tendency to turn back toward sin because you still have the "flesh." The flesh is the infection that we all received at birth. It is the tendency to sin. We are commanded not to live according to the flesh (Gal. 5:13–21). But alone, without any accountability, we will fail. We need the strength and accountability that the body of Christ provides.

Submit yourself to the wisdom of others in the church and let them speak deeply into your life. And you know what makes this a lot easier? *You* initiate it. You place yourself under the authority of others, giving them permission to correct you when you stray. You are the only one who can make yourself accountable to others.

Spiritual Gifts

You have a gift given to you by the Holy Spirit that he wants you to use in the church. The Holy Spirit alone distributes "spiritual gifts," according to his will (1 Cor. 12:11). I don't know which one you have, but you need to find out. Why? Who wants to live each day without an eye, tooth, nose, or pinky toe? The Bible speaks about spiritual gifts four times: Romans 12, 1 Corinthians 12, 1 Peter 4, and Ephesians 4. (These are easy to remember: two twelves and two fours.) Here is the basic list of gifts given in the Bible (see 1 Corinthians 12–14; Rom. 12:3–8; Eph. 4:11–12; 1 Pet. 4:10–11):

Serving: doing behind-the-scenes work
Teaching: educating others in the Christian worldview
Exhortation: building people up through words of
    encouragement
Giving: liberally giving finances to the needs of the body
Leadership: guiding and directing others
Administration: taking care of organizational issues
Mercy: being there for people who are in need of a friend

Evangelism: spreading the good news of the gospel with great effectiveness

Pastor: leading the church through teaching and vision

Word of wisdom: a prophetic word that gives sage advice from God

Word of knowledge: a prophetic word that provides divine information

Faith: the ability to believe more deeply, carrying the church through difficulties

Gifts of healing: the divine ability to heal in a supernatural way

Miracles: the ability to perform miracles for the edification of the body and for evangelism

Distinguishing between spirits: the supernatural ability to discern when something is from Satan

Tongues: the ability to worship in a prayer language or the ability to speak in a language unknown to the speaker for the purpose of evangelism

Interpretation of tongues: the ability to interpret when people speak in tongues for the edification of the body

Prophecy: directly speaking on behalf of God, giving divine revelation

Apostleship: the divine authority to establish and lead the church based upon personal witness of Christ's resurrection

The lists given in Scripture are probably not meant to exhaust the ways that God has gifted his body; they are representative. In fact, I read one theologian who listed martyrdom as a gift of the Spirit. Now that is a gift you can only use once! Many of these gifts are controversial. Some believe that the more miraculous gifts, such as tongues, prophecy, and healings, ceased once the apostles died. I encourage you to look into that debate, though we will not discuss it here. There are good people on both sides. But what you need to do is discover your gift. How do you do that? This acronym might help:

G Give yourself to God.

I Involve yourself in various ministries.

F Focus on a specific gift.

T Talk to others about your gift.

S Seek God's guidance.

One thing is certain: these gifts are given for the edification of the body (1 Cor. 12:7). That means you cannot use them alone.

Encouragement

We can't do it alone. Do what? Life! As we will see in the next chapter, life is hard, and it does not necessarily get easier when you become a believer. We must have encouragement from others or our fire will go out. In order to do this, you must be transparent with others. Let your brothers and sisters get to know you. Let them get to know the *real* you. Once everyone is real, everyone can be encouraged together. The body of Christ is the place for lifting each other up. My biological sisters are my greatest encouragers. They encourage simply because they know the real me and they stick around. And trust me, if you knew the real me you would know how hard that is! You have many brothers and sisters in the body of Christ who can encourage you, lift you up when you are down, come to your aid when you are in need, and feed your dog when you are out of town. And you must be humble enough to accept this encouragement.

Now that you are a Christian, you should involve yourself

in the lives of others. Continually look for ways to encourage them. Be there for them when no one else will. This life is too crazy to go it alone.

WRONG ATTITUDES TOWARD CHURCH

Please allow me to preemptively discharge some of the wrong attitudes you may have about church or attitudes you've seen in others. These wrong attitudes can cause you to become one of the following.

Nomadic Christian. This is a Christian who travels from church to church, never settling down, never committing. This is easy to do because, for many of us, there are so many churches to choose from. There is nothing wrong with visiting many churches (in fact, I suggest it), but there is a point where you have to settle down in your "home church." Nomadic Christians never can join in true fellowship the way God desires.

Exclusive Christian. This is a Christian who believes that his church is the only true church and that all other churches are false churches. This is a dangerous way to think. We do want to be discerning about other churches, but we don't want to be overly critical and exclusive. Many churches are different, both in belief and practice. But if they have belief and focus on the central issues—the person and work of Christ—they are a true church. Different? Yes. False? No. Exclusive Christians usually have a very small circle of fellowship due to their critical spirit. Don't be this way.

Inclusive Christian. This is the opposite of the exclusive Christian. This person does not really care who he fellowships with. To him, the body of Christ is made up of any who simply claim to be Christian. Many churches don't care about doctrine or how you live. These are not Christian churches. They are country clubs with no ability to truly edify you in the Lord. If you are at an inclusive church, find a new one.

Burned Christian. This Christian does not go to church because he had a bad experience or two in the past. My advice: get over it! We are dealing with sinful people. Have grace. Have mercy. Have forgiveness. People are going to let you down left and right, even in the church. If you get burned in church, look at it as an opportunity to forgive and let it go to God. We should be more than willing to put up with the failures of our spiritual family.

Consumer Christian. This person says, "It's all about me." This person only wants the church to serve him. He goes to church to get, not to give. If you have this attitude, I promise you will be insatiable and unsatisfied. The most satisfying thing we can do as Christians is to give. The consumer Christian just wants to know what others can do for him. I want you to only seek what you can do for others.

ONE ANOTHER

This thing called *church* is not about a building, steeple, sermon, or minister. It is about "one another." It is about holding each other up in grace and wisdom. It is about loving each other. It is about not being alone. It is about submission. It is about a common Father. It is about celebration. It is about fellowship. God loves *koinonia*. In fact, he has been in eternal *koinonia* in the Trinity. The Father, Son, and Holy Spirit have shared with us a wonderful gift—the drive to be in relationship with others. I want to conclude this chapter by overwhelming you with many of the "one another" commands in Scripture.

- Love one another (Rom. 12:10).
- Outdo one another in showing honor (Rom. 12:10).

- Be of the same mind with one another (Rom. 12:16).
- Let us not judge one another (Rom. 14:13).
- Build up one another (Rom. 14:19).
- Accept one another (Rom. 15:7).
- Instruct one another (Rom. 15:14).
- Serve one another (Gal. 5:13).
- Put up with one another (Eph. 4:2).
- Be subject to one another (Eph. 5:21).
- Forgive one another (Eph. 4:32).
- Think of one another more significantly than yourself (Phil. 2:3).
- Do not lie to one another (Col. 3:9).
- Admonish one another (Col. 3:16).
- Comfort one another (1 Thess. 4:18).
- Encourage one another (1 Thess. 5:11).
- Live in peace with one another (1 Thess. 5:13).
- Stimulate one another to love (Heb. 10:24).
- Pray for one another (James 5:16).
- Confess your sins to one another (James 5:16).
- Be hospitable to one another (1 Pet. 4:9).
- Serve one another (1 Pet. 4:10).
- Have fellowship with one another (1 John 1:7).

There are over fifty of these "one anothering" verses. Ask yourself, is it possible to obey these if you are on your own and not in relationship with other believers?

DISCUSSION QUESTIONS

1. The church is your new family. Since it is a family, name some things that you will have to put up with.
2. Why is it so hard to be accountable to someone else? What things can you do right now to overcome your fears?
3. Why do you think it is important to God that we take the Lord's Supper together?

4. Many Christians neglect gathering together with one another. You may be tempted to do the same. Why do you sometimes make up an excuse for not going to church?

5. What do you think your spiritual gift is? Explain.

ADDITIONAL DISCIPLESHIP TRAINING

Church: Why Bother?, Philip Yancey

Ecclesiology and Eschatology, part 6 of The Theology Program, Credo House Ministries

What's So Spiritual about Your Gifts?, Henry Blackaby and Mel Blackaby

9

Suffering

When my children were little, they liked to pray at the dinner table. They would say, "Thank you, God, for making me." What a great and simple prayer! Children seem to be able to recognize the simplicity and glory of life more than adults. When we become adults, things change quite a bit. We approach God broken, bruised, and scarred. Sometimes we are not too sure that we are thankful that God made us.

I love life. I really do. On my best days I thank God for making me. I would much rather exist than not exist. Seems pretty elemental, doesn't it? Well, not really. Why? Because life is hard. And dare I say that the Christian life may be harder. If you signed up for this thing called "Christianity" to get an easy ride through life as God swoops in and takes care of all your problems, you signed up for the wrong ride. You see, from the outside looking in, Christians don't have it much different from non-Christians when it comes to pain and suffering.

Not long ago I received a letter from a skeptic of Christianity. He made the following observation: "It sure doesn't look like believers are getting any special payoff in this life. Is there any evidence to show that Christians that pray to their God for better protection from harm are better protected than we, the infidels?"

My answer: No, there is not. But whoever said there would be? We are Christians not because of any "payoff" in this life, but because Christ rose from the grave and we have nowhere else to go (John 6:68). The payoff is that our enmity with the Creator of the universe who loves us has been resolved. The payoff is our hope for the final restoration of all things when Christ comes back. But, in this life, it does not seem that Christians have any less suffering and pain.

Here are some examples:

- The divorce rate among professing Christians and non-Christians is about the same.
- The percentage of Christians who get cancer is the same as the percentage of non-Christians.
- The death rate of Christians and non-Christians is the same:
  - 1 out of 1 Christians who tithe die.
  - 1 out of 1 Christians who pray regularly die.
  - 1 out of 1 Christians who go to church regularly die.
  - 1 out of 1 Christians die.
  - 1 out of 1 non-Christians die.

The greatest heroes of the Christian faith are undoubtedly the apostles of Christ. They were the ones specially commissioned to establish the gospel all over the world. They serve as good examples about what God lets his family go through. What do their lives look like with regard to pain and suffering? It depends on your perspective. If you think God does not will for his children to experience sickness, pain, trouble, rejection, and untimely deaths, then the apostles will be a fly in your ointment; their lives (and deaths) won't make sense. You may even have your faith disillusioned. But if you understand that God, for his own good reasons, wills for even the worst type of pain and suffering to saturate the lives of believers, then your faith won't be affected too much. Below is a list of what happened to the apostles. We get this information primarily through the early church fathers who wrote after the apostles died. Some of the traditions are more stable than others, but is seems clear that almost all the apostles died a gruesome martyr's death.

1. James was killed with a sword (AD 45).
2. Peter was hung on a cross head downward (AD 64).
3. Andrew was hung from an olive tree (AD 70).
4. Thomas was thrust through with spears (AD 70).
5. Philip was crucified (AD 54).
6. Matthew was beheaded (AD 65).
7. Nathanael was crucified (AD 70).
8. James, the brother of the Lord, was thrown from the top of the temple in Jerusalem (AD 63).
9. Simon the Zealot was crucified (AD 74).
10. Judas Thaddeus was beaten with sticks (AD 72).
11. Matthias was stoned on a cross (AD 70).
12. John died a natural death (AD 95).
13. Paul was beheaded (AD 69).

You get the picture? There is really no way to avoid pain, suffering, and evil. We live in a fallen, broken world that is diseased by sin. God is content to leave it this way until Christ comes back.

SURPRISED BY SUFFERING

The majority of Christians who suffer with significant doubts in their faith do so due to the pain and suffering they experience. The late Christian philosopher Ronald Nash said in a lecture titled "Christian Apologetics" that it is completely irrational to reject the Christian faith for any other reason than the problem of evil. This expresses the respect that he gave this issue.

The "problem of evil" is the problem of pain and suffering, and it is indeed a tremendous problem. Great Christian writer C. S. Lewis wrote an academic book on pain, suffering, and evil called *The Problem of Pain*. It is a wonderful, monumental work, and I recommend it without hesitation. But after he wrote this book, he *experienced* pain and suffering at a different level. It is one thing to evaluate something from the outside; it is quite another to personally experience it. C. S. Lewis lost his wife after a battle with cancer that had been filled with ups and downs. It broke him and brought him to his knees. Lewis rested for a while in front of God, asking questions from his disillusionment. Thankfully, this whole experience is recorded in another book about pain. *A Grief Observed* is Lewis's personal account of laying himself bare before God, expressing his confusion. I highly recommend this book as well.

I don't want you to be surprised by suffering. I want you to be able to handle evil and pain both in an academic way and an emotional way. First, let's look at the academic side of evil, pain, and suffering, often called the *intellectual problem of evil*.

THE INTELLECTUAL PROBLEM OF EVIL

The intellectual problem of evil attempts to use logic to explain a world that has pain, suffering, and evil, yet also has a good, all-powerful God who rules it. Let me define this problem by using a syllogism:

Premise 1: God is all-good (omnibenevolent).
Premise 2: God is all-powerful (omnipotent).

Premise 3: Suffering and evil exist.
Why wouldn't an all-powerful God who is all-good stop
    suffering and evil from existing?

This problem of evil has only intensified in a world where technology allows us to share in the sufferings of millions of people all over the earth. The Internet brings us one click away from faces of those who have had their children kidnapped, are starving to death, are diseased and deformed in unimaginable ways, and who have had loveless parents leave them locked in a closet as they go out to dinner. We can't go a day without hearing about evils that are common to the human race.

We understandably begin to question God's role in all of this. If God exists, if God is good and does not like evil, and if God is powerful enough to change things, why does evil still exist? Let me give you some of the *wrong* ways people handle this issue.

The Sadotheistic Response

Premise 1: God is all-good (omnibenevolent).
Premise 2: God is all-powerful (omnipotent).
Premise 3: Suffering and evil exist.
Conclusion: God enjoys bringing about suffering and
    pain for no reason at all.

God is on an opposing team.

The sadotheist believes that God is an evil sadist who enjoys bringing about suffering with no good intentions whatsoever. This could be true. It *could* be the case that God is a sadist. What I mean is that there is no logical difficulty that cannot be overcome. The problem with the sadotheist position is that this is not how God has revealed himself in history or in the

Bible. The cross of Christ is the greatest illustration of God's love that we have. God himself got his feet dirty and his hands bloody in order to save mankind. On top of this, the sadotheist has to borrow from God's morality to judge God! In other words, how does the sadotheist know what good and evil are outside of God's love and existence? This view, while logically possible, is biblically wrong.

Open Theistic Response

> Premise 1: God is all-good (omnibenevolent).
> Premise 2: God is all-powerful (omnipotent).
> Premise 3: Suffering and evil exist.
> Conclusion: God has self-limited his abilities so that he can truly relate to mankind. Therefore God *cannot* stop all suffering and evil.

God is on our team, but he is only a cheerleader on the sidelines, rooting for us as he watches things unfold.

The open theist handles the problem of pain and suffering by saying that God, due to his commitment to man's freedom, *can't* do anything about it. This is a self-limiting both of his power and his knowledge. Evil may happen, but it is only because God is committed to the freedom of man's will. This view is logically possible as well. In other words, God could, more or less, have a hands-off approach to what happens in the world. But this militates against much of Scripture, which says that God is in control and he does know the future. For example, look at what the book of Daniel says about this:

> All the inhabitants of the earth are accounted as nothing,
>   and he does according to his will among the host of
>   heaven

and among the inhabitants of the earth;
and none can stay his hand
or say to him, "What have you done?" (Dan. 4:35)

It looks like God is in control of things. Whatever happens is in some sense God's will, even evil. I think it is important for us, at this point (as your eyebrows raise and your heartbeat increases!), to distinguish between what theologians call "the two wills of God." God has two wills. We call them his "will of decree" and his "will of desire." Does God want you to suffer? Yes. Does God want you to suffer? No. These are both right! Let's put it this way: Did God will that his Son be killed on the cross? Yes. Did God will that his Son die on the cross? No. You see, there is a sense in which God's *ultimate* desire or will is that no one ever sin or suffer evil. But in a fallen world, God uses sin to accomplish his purpose. If God did not use sin and evil, then he would not be involved, for there is nothing else to work with! He has to get his hands dirty, if you will, and use sin if he is to accomplish his good purpose. Ultimately, this leads to a world without sin and suffering. But for now, he works with it and, in a contextualized sense, wills it. The open theist response to evil fails to see how God could be involved in such terrible things. But it also fails to consider that God is working all things together for good, even suffering and pain: "And we know that for those who love God all things work together for good, for those who are called according to his purpose" (Rom. 8:28).

The Pantheistic Response

Premise 1: God is all-good (omnibenevolent).
Premise 2: God is all-powerful (omnipotent).
Premise 3: Suffering and evil exist.

> Conclusion: Suffering and evil is an illusion that we
>> create with our own mind. To eradicate it, we must
>> deny its existence.

God is not on any team, since there really is no opposition.

The pantheistic view tells us to close our eyes and ears and act as if evil, suffering, and pain do not really exist. In this view, all suffering is an illusion that we must train ourselves to be blind to. But this does not work, rationally or biblically. To *deny* the existence of something does not *determine* the existence of something. The Bible speaks very clearly about the existence of evil. As we saw in chapter 6, Jesus instructs us in the Disciples' Prayer to request deliverance "from evil." Would he command us to pray against something that does not exist? I don't think so. Therefore, the pantheistic response is not a Christian option, either.

The Atheistic Response

> Premise 1: God is all-good (omnibenevolent).
> Premise 2: God is all-powerful (omnipotent).
> Premise 3: Suffering and evil exist.
> Conclusion: An all-good, all-powerful God cannot exist,
>> since there is so much suffering and evil in the
>> world. If he did exist, he would eradicate this evil.

God is not on any team, because he does not exist.

The atheistic response looks reasonable on the surface, but when we take a closer look, it is logically absurd. First (and most importantly), like the sadotheist, in order to define the very concept of "evil," the atheist has to borrow from a theistic worldview (one that believes in God). In other words, if there is no God, there is no such thing as evil. Second, if there is a problem of evil, there is also a problem of good. If there is no God, how do we explain the good that happens in the world? In the atheistic worldview, there is actually no such thing as good or evil. This, itself, does not make atheism wrong (there are many other arguments that do), but it does show the absurdity of *this* argument. Finally (and read this carefully), *the one who believes in God has to explain the existence of evil; the atheist has to explain the existence of everything else.* Which is easier?

The Christian Response

Premise 1: God is all-good (omnibenevolent).

Premise 2: God is all-powerful (omnipotent).

Premise 3: Suffering and evil exist.

Conclusion: God has good reasons for allowing suffering and evil to exist. He uses suffering and evil to accomplish a greater good, *even if we never know exactly what that reason is.*

God is on our team, and he is both the quarterback and coach!

You see, the "intellectual problem of evil" is not really a problem—if by *problem*, you mean that it cannot be solved, rationally or biblically. Rationally, there is no reason to assume that God cannot have a purpose for evil that results in good. We see this every day. When someone has brain surgery, he has to endure the intense suffering of having his skin cut and skull taken apart. But the greater good of having a tumor removed is evident to all. There is no reason to say that God can't use even the most atrocious suffering to bring about a greater good.

This is also clear biblically. Not only does Roman 8:28 say that God works all things together for good (and this most certainly includes evil), but many stories in the Bible demonstrate this truth. For example, in the book of Genesis, Joseph, who loved and followed God, was sold into slavery by his very own brothers (chap. 37). After he was wrongly imprisoned for many years, he was finally released and elevated to a position second only to Pharaoh (41:39). While in this position, Joseph made it possible for most of the world, including his father and brothers, to live through the famine that lasted seven years (41:56–57). God intended to use Joseph's suffering to bring about good. Notice what Joseph said to his sorrowful brothers: "As for you, you meant evil against me, but God meant it for good, to bring it about that many people should be kept alive, as they are today" (Gen. 50:20).

"God meant it for good." Therefore, the intellectual problem of evil can be dealt with without losing intellectual integrity. In fact, as we look through the options, the Christian option is the option that makes the *most* rational sense.

But this does not make it a slam dunk. Intellect is one thing. Emotions are another.

THE EMOTIONAL PROBLEM OF EVIL

Let's face it, the problem of suffering, pain, and evil has very little to do with logic. Suffering and pain are very emotional. We can be logically prepared to give an answer for these troubles, but it is hard to be emotionally prepared to give answers, either to ourselves or others. When evil touches our lives, we collapse emotionally. When we are in the throes of pain, the tears we shed before God are not produced from our minds, but from our hearts.

Let me get personal for a bit.

My sister committed suicide on January 4, 2004. It was traumatic for our whole family. It did not come as a surprise, as we had suffered with her in her depression for a year and a half before she finally succeeded in ending her life. I performed her funeral, which, as you can imagine, was incredibly hard. But I was more emotionally stable than you might think. I preached on the problem of pain in relation to my sister's depression and death. I had all the answers that day. My mother did not handle Angie's death well at all. She blamed herself. She lived with tears filling her heart and overwhelming her body for two years. Her blood pressure was high and she hardly slept. In 2006, at the age of 56, she suffered a ruptured brain aneurysm. She lived, but received from God the mentality of a child and was completely paralyzed on her left side. She now sits in one chair all day long watching the same movies over and over. We have to change her diaper, feed her, and transfer her anytime she needs to be moved. These events caused significant depression in my family. One sister went into a deep despair. My father blames himself for everything and can't recover. Through all of this, my emotions were rock solid. I thought to myself, "This is how Christians should handle things. If they have good theology, everything will be all right."

I held this attitude until March 15, 2010. At 12:01 p.m. that day, I broke. I don't know how or why, but my mind was lost. I went into significant depression for six straight weeks. Nothing I could think or do would "snap me out of it" (which had been my advice to people before this event). I suppose that all the troubles had piled up at some place in my mind and finally found a way of escape. I held onto God, but just barely. Rather, he held onto me. It was the emotional problem of evil made incarnate in my life, and I did not know what to do.

The emotional problem of evil amounts to the difficulty of bearing the weight of the troubles that are handed to us. When we are broken, the problem is realized. It is no longer a logical thing; it becomes an issue of the heart that cries out to God in unbearable suffering and says, "Help me!" or "My God, my God, why have you forsaken me?" When the help does not come, the emotional problem of evil is experienced and defined.

The best thing I can tell you is that God is with you through all the sufferings that you might experience. He is with me now. He never guaranteed or promised that life would be easy. I lean on those who, throughout Scripture and the history of the church, experienced worse suffering, yet maintained their love and trust in God.

We must be prepared for the troubles that will surely come. The following Scriptures speak to our suffering:

> For this light momentary affliction is preparing for us an eternal weight of glory beyond all comparison. (2 Cor. 4:17)

> But he has said to me, "My grace is sufficient for you, for my power is made perfect in weakness." Therefore I will boast all the more gladly of my weaknesses, so that the power of Christ may rest upon me. For the sake of Christ, then, I am content with weaknesses, insults, hardships, persecutions, and calamities. For when I am weak, then I am strong. (2 Cor. 12:9–10)

> Not only that, but we rejoice in our sufferings, knowing that suffering produces endurance. (Rom. 5:3)

> Count it all joy, my brothers, when you meet trials of various kinds, for you know that the testing of your faith produces steadfastness. (James 1:2–3)

> In this you rejoice, though now for a little while, if necessary, you have been grieved by various trials. (1 Pet. 1:6)

Beloved, do not be surprised at the fiery trial when it comes upon you to test you, as though something strange were happening to you. But rejoice insofar as you share Christ's sufferings, that you may also rejoice and be glad when his glory is revealed. (1 Pet. 4:12–13)

Resist [the Devil], firm in your faith, knowing that the same kinds of suffering are being experienced by your brotherhood throughout the world. (1 Pet. 5:9)

The entire Old Testament book of Job is devoted to the problem of evil. Job was struck deeply by the emotional problem of evil. God took his family, possessions, and health. At one point, Job cursed the day of his birth (3:1–3). Why did God do this? Why did Job have to endure such suffering and pain? We, as readers, know that God was allowing his faith to be tested. But Job never knew why.

One of my best friends from childhood was at my sister Angie's funeral. He came to my mother's house after the funeral for the time of fellowship and mourning among friends and family. He and I had been talking for months about Christianity prior to this. I was trying to convince him to become a Christian. I felt that we were really close to getting there. While we were at my mother's house, he timidly waited to talk to me. After saying he was sorry about the death of my sister, he asked the key question: "Michael, I am really close to becoming a Christian. I actually believe it all. But I am scared." "Scared of what?" I responded. "I am scared of what God will do to my children. Your mom is the best Christian that I know. And look what God did to her. He took Angie from her. I guess what I am asking is this: will God protect my children?"

I did not have a good answer for my friend that day. That

is, I did not have a "good" one so long as you define *good* as something that is attractive from the world's standpoint. I did have a *right* answer: "I don't know." That was my answer to him and that is my answer to you. I don't know if God will protect you or your children. I don't know if God will protect your spouse, friends, mom, dad, or siblings. I don't know if he will protect *you*. The word *protect* in this sense is limited. God will give us all we need to accomplish his purpose during our short stay here on the earth. I suspect that you will go through many trials, experience much evil, and suffer physically in this life. I suspect that your heart will break many times and you will shed many tears. Christians experience every kind of suffering, including the following:

> Physical: pain, cancer, accidents, disease, etc.
> Emotional: depression, anxiety, etc.
> Financial: bankruptcy, poverty, bad business deals, etc.
> Spiritual: sin, God's hiddenness and silence, etc.
> Meaningless: stubbing a toe, minor irritations, weight
>   problems, car accidents, etc.
> Referred: suffering of others

But take courage. More than likely you will also experience great joy and happiness. Maybe you will be spared of much of the suffering and pain described here. But the fact is that Christians can and do experience tremendous suffering. You can find joy through it all so long as you know that God is in it. He has a purpose. Sometimes this purpose has great and wonderful effects that we can see. Sometimes his purpose is hidden in the darkness of heaven. Sometimes God puts us through trials with a simple purpose: that we believe. You see, maintaining the integrity of your belief when the storms come glorifies God incredibly. Often, this is God's only purpose. It is between you and him. When you suffer, are you going to be surprised and raise your fist at God and say, "How could you?" or are you going to maintain your belief and trust in him, knowing he has this under control? That is what pain and suffering come down to. Trusting God in the midst of pain and suffering may be the greatest expression of worship that we can accomplish here on earth.

I know it has been hard to work through this chapter. If we could change the color of the pages, these pages would be dark. But this issue is so important for your discipleship; it is a problem that often causes Christians to stumble. I pray that in your sufferings you will not be surprised, but you will turn to our sovereign Lord, knowing that he has a purpose—even if you never know what it is. And know that he loves you greatly. I also pray that in your happiness, you can thank God for making you. It is a good thing to be alive, and one day he will wipe every tear from our eyes: "He will wipe away every tear from their eyes, and death shall be no more, neither shall there be mourning, nor crying, nor pain anymore, for the former things have passed away" (Rev. 21:4).

Enjoy life without anxiety, knowing that God brings about both pain and joy for his often mysterious reasons: "In the day of prosperity be joyful, and in the day of adversity consider: God has made the one as well as the other, so that man may not find out anything that will be after him" (Eccles. 7:14).

DISCUSSION QUESTIONS

1. Why do you think God allows so much suffering in the world?
2. Express ways in which you have been confused by suffering.

3. What are some of the seemingly "meaningless" sufferings that happen to you on a daily basis? Why might God allow them?
4. Further critique the atheist solution to the problem of evil.
5. How can you prepare yourself now for the effect of the emotional problem of evil once it comes into your life?

ADDITIONAL DISCIPLESHIP TRAINING

Dark Night of the Soul, St. John of the Cross

Suffering and the Sovereignty of God, John Piper and Justin Taylor, eds.

When God Weeps, Joni Eareckson Tada and Steve Estes

Where Is God When It Hurts?, Phillip Yancy

10

Mission

I don't remember much of my younger years, especially before I was ten. Nobody really does, except those who have hyperthymesia (the bizarre ability to remember every autobiographical event of your life). But one of my earliest memories is from when I was four. I was swinging with my best friend in our neighborhood. While pushing his swing, I asked, "Todd, do you believe in Jesus?" He responded, "No." "Then you are going to hell," I immediately said. "Then I do," was his quick response. Well, that was easy. He was a Christian, right? After this, I don't think I ever talked to him about God again. From my perspective, my job was complete. This is called *evangelism*. It may not be very effective evangelism, but it was the attempt of a four-year-old to introduce a friend to Jesus so that he could join the family.

My goal in this last chapter is to send you off on a mission for Christ. My goal is to prepare you to spread the *gospel* (more on that word in a bit). We are on this earth only for a short time. From eternity's perspective, we're here for a *very* short time. In my childhood Sunday school classes, I heard it expressed this way: Compare eternity to an ant walking around the entire earth until it drives a path so deep that the earth splits in two. It would take quite a while, wouldn't it? Your time here on earth is that first step! Get the picture? In truth, this illustration does not really work. To be more accurate, the earth and eternity we have waiting for us would *never* split in two (and in real life, the ant could never accomplish this, because the path would be covered over and over by natural means). The point is that our stay here on earth is but a breath, and this makes the opportunity for our mission very short. The Bible puts it this way: "Behold, you have made my days a few handbreadths, and my lifetime is as nothing before you. Surely all mankind stands as a mere breath! *Selah*" (Ps. 39:5).

THE GREAT COMMISSION

We get the idea of *mission* from Christ. After he was resurrected, Christ sent his apostles on a mission. This mission is most clearly explained in the Gospel of Matthew:

> And Jesus came and said to them, "All authority in heaven and on earth has been given to me. Go therefore and make disciples of all nations, baptizing them in the name of the Father and of the Son and of the Holy Spirit, teaching them to observe all that I have commanded you. And behold, I am with you always, to the end of the age." (Matt. 28:18–20)

These are Christ's last words in the book of Matthew. Usually, last words are significant. We call this passage "The Great Commission." According to Merriam-Webster, a *commission* is the "authority to act for, in behalf of, or in place of another." I think this definition works for this passage. We are given the authority to act for Christ. But more than that, we are given the mandate to do this. This is our mission on our short "one step" stay here on the earth.

As we go through the last words of Christ in the Gospel of Matthew one phrase at a time, understand that these are Christ's words to *you*. This is your Great Commission.

"All Authority in Heaven and on Earth Has Been Given to Me"

This statement is more than just a prologue to something better. This is the best news. The Great Commission is meaningless and impotent without it. All authority in the entire universe was given to Jesus. This has tremendous implications for our life and mission. You see, before Christ accomplished what he did on the cross, before Christ's resurrection from the dead, he did not have "all authority." When he was conceived by the Holy Spirit in the virgin Mary, he laid aside his authority by taking on the divine mission to save us by becoming human (Phil. 2:6–8). He did not lay aside his *divinity* (which is impossible); he laid aside his *authority*. Now that Christ has accomplished redemption by living the perfect life, dying, and rising from the grave, he has reestablished his sovereign dominion over the entire universe.

What does this mean for you? It means that the eternal, all-powerful, undisputed, all-knowing God, Jesus Christ, has your back! It means that you have the resources to complete what Christ asks you to complete. Most importantly, it means that you don't have to rely on your own power to accomplish what Christ mandates. Take courage; the mission we have has a powerful benefactor!

"Go Therefore and Make Disciples of All Nations"

First, notice the "therefore." As any good biblical scholar would tell you, when you see a "therefore" go find out what it is there for! *Therefore* is an adverb that means "for this reason" or "because of." The command to "go" is based on Christ's authority that has been given to him. "Because I have been given all authority and power," Christ says, "go and make disciples of all nations."

Second, notice that Christ does not say, "Go and make converts." He does not even say, "Go and evangelize." Our mission is to make *disciples* of Christ by the power and authority of Christ. A disciple is a committed follower of someone. You become a disciple of Christ when you submit your life to him. When I talked to my friend Todd on the swing set, all I did (in an insufficient way) was try to make him a convert. I said, "Do you believe in Jesus?" His "yes" was all I needed to write "mission accomplished" across his forehead. But the mission was *not* accomplished. It had only begun. Of course, part of the mission is to share Jesus and have people come to a point where they trust Jesus (which I don't suppose Todd really did), but the mission is so much more. Making disciples is a lifelong process. It is not just making converts.

"Baptizing Them in the Name of the Father and of the Son and of the Holy Spirit"

In our mission, baptism is the first step in becoming a disciple. Why does Jesus say to baptize? What is so important about being dunked underwater by someone (or sprinkled over the head—but this is not the time for *that* debate!)? Primarily, baptism is a vivid illustration of our entrance into the family of God. In Christ's day, baptism was more broadly used and understood than it is today. But even today, other religions have people baptized into their faith. It symbolizes a washing and renewal. When people are baptized into Christianity, they are not just becoming a part of the family, they are expressing to others their joy and commitment in becoming a disciple of Christ. Because Jesus commends baptism, I encourage you to get baptized if you have not done so already.

Christ also said that we are to be baptized in the "name of the Father and of the Son and of the Holy Spirit." What a great and explicit reference to the Trinity. None of the members of the Trinity are left out. They are all equal and separate. When you are baptized or baptize others, you are baptizing them into a *Trinitarian* faith.

"Teaching Them to Observe All That I Have Commanded You"

Only two actions are required for making disciples: baptizing and teaching. Christ says that we are to "teach them" all that he has commanded. That is a lot of stuff. The four Gospels (Matthew, Mark, Luke, and John) all contain a great deal of information on Christ and what he commanded. And by extension, since they are inspired, the "all" includes all of the New Testament and Old Testament. We can never exhaust all the teaching of Christ or the Bible. However, this is what we are commanded to do. It is a never-ending process. You are commanded to teach. In order to teach, you have to know. This means you must stay in the Word. You are to be a student of Scripture.

Teaching by using words is a great and necessary thing. But making disciples is more than just speaking truth with your mouth. Your life can be just as much a witness to your faith as preaching a sermon. People watch how you live. They watch for years. If you live in such a way that is pleasing to the Lord, then people will be sponges to your life. They will want to be like you. They will see your faith through your life.

Remember: you have to gain an audience for your words to be endeared. Your kindness, grace, transparency, and hope will eventually affect those whom God is calling to himself. Beating them over the head with your words can be frustrating and countereffective. You have to wait until the time is right. Teach others by your words *and* your life. And remember, there is a *lot* to teach. Be patient with people. The power of Christ is mediated through the power of the Holy Spirit. And he often does not work as fast as we would like. The discipleship process of teaching people is a lifelong joy, not an overnight success.

"And Behold, I Am with You Always, to the End of the Age."

What a great and comforting ending. Christ begins by basing our mission on his authority and power, and he ends by expressing his commitment *to us*, the disciplers. The Great Commission is bookended with Christ's involvement. Christ will never leave us. His hands are holding us up during our short mission on earth.

THE GOSPEL

I want you to spread the gospel. But what is the gospel? What are you supposed to tell people? You would be surprised at how many different answers people give.

The word *gospel* is taken from the Greek word *euangelion*. It is the word we get *evangelism* and *evangelical* from. Its meaning is simple. It translates to "good news." The gospel is the good news of Christ. What about Christ? Everything! From his love and grace to his judgment and renewal, from the incarnation to the resurrection, the gospel is the good news of God's activity on behalf of man.

We use the word *gospel* in three primary ways:

1. Gospels. Sometimes we say "the Gospels." This refers to the first four books of the New Testament: Matthew, Mark, Luke, and John. They are called the Gospels because all of them tell the same story about what Christ did here on earth, but from four different perspectives.

2. Gospel. Sometimes we use the word *gospel* to refer to everything God has done for us. Paul, in the book of Romans, teaches gospel throughout the entire epistle. This includes everything from the universal sinfulness of man to the choosing of God's elect. From beginning to end, everything that God has revealed is good news for those who trust him.

3. Essential gospel. Sometimes the word *gospel* refers to the *essence* of the good news. In other words, it is what you learn and understand in order to be saved. When I asked my friend Todd if he believed in Jesus, this was a good start. My bold proclamation that he was going to hell if he did not believe was true, but it was not quite the whole story. You see, I did not tell him who Jesus was or what Jesus did. Just the handle "Jesus" communicates very little. So what was I supposed to tell him about Jesus? What are the essentials that we must believe in order to become a child of God?

Paul says that there are parts of the gospel that are of "first importance." Listen to what he says about the essential gospel:

> Now I would remind you, brothers, of the gospel I preached to you, which you received, in which you stand, and by which you are being saved, if you hold fast to the word I preached to you—unless you believed in vain. For I delivered to you as *of first importance* what I also received: that Christ died for our sins in accordance with the Scriptures, that he was buried, that he was raised on the third day in accordance with the Scriptures. (1 Cor. 15:1–4)

Paul believed that some things are more important than others. The debate about whether Christ turned water into wine or grape juice (John 2:1–10) is interesting and is part of the gospel story, but it is not the essence of the gospel. I don't ask people first and foremost to agree with my interpretation of this matter. There are things that are more important. They are of *first* importance.

Before further examining 1 Corinthians 15, allow me to push you in your discipleship in this area. The entire story of Christ is the good news, but there are essentials and nonessentials to the Christian faith. There are some things that we as Christians should divide over, and there are many things that we should not divide over. Figure 10.1 illustrates this. I call it "the concentric circle of importance."

Fig. 10.1 The Concentric Circle of Importance

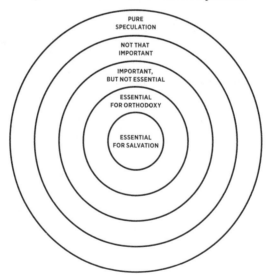

Essential for Salvation. Some things *must* be believed in order to be saved. There is no debate about them, and Scripture clearly teaches that they are essential. My list would include: belief in God; belief that Christ is the divine Son of God; belief that Christ died for our sins; belief that we are sinners in need of saving; belief that Christ rose from the grave; and, implied in all the others, belief that faith in Christ is necessary for those who can believe (this excludes infants, the mentally unable, and those who die in their mothers' wombs). I think that covers it.

These are what Paul refers to as being "of first importance": "That Christ died for our sins in accordance with the Scriptures, that he was buried, that he was raised on the third day in accordance with the Scriptures." The essentials are all about the person and work of Christ.

Essential for Orthodoxy. Some issues are extremely important and are a part of the historic Christian faith, but are not necessarily essential for one to believe before they can be saved. These are those issues that Christians *do not* divide over. They include the essentials for salvation, but extend beyond them. There are too many to list, but let me give you some examples: the doctrine of the Trinity, the hypostatic union, the inspiration of Scripture, the details concerning the second coming of Christ, belief in creation *ex nihilo* ("out of nothing"), belief in the omniscience of God, belief in the sanctity of life, and belief in the marriage bed being limited to one man and one woman. The early church called the essentials for orthodoxy the *regula fidei.* This means "the rule of faith." These are the things that have been believed "always, everywhere, and by all." In other words, new discoveries or ideas can never militate against these nor find their way into this category. Another expression you might hear is, "If it is true, it's not new; if it is new, it's not true." I don't think we have to go that far. There can be new thoughts that contribute to a better understanding of the Christian faith, but that might not be considered essential.

Important, but Not Essential. Some issues Christians can have great debates over, but should not divide over. They include people's views on predestination (unconditional or conditional), the age of the earth, the exact details of the second coming, whether there are modern-day prophets, issues of church government, and the age at which a person can be baptized. As passionate as you may be about some of these subjects, do not divide over them. But just as importantly, know this: *nonessential does not mean unimportant.* These are indeed very important. They just need to be put in their proper place on the concentric circle.

Not That Important. Some issues are interesting but don't affect our faith that much. For example: Which Gospel was written first? Did Paul write two other letters to the Corinthians? Should we have musical instruments in the church? Who wrote the book of Hebrews? From where did Peter write his letters? Exactly how did Judas die?

Pure Speculation. Some issues don't make any difference at all. Do angels have wings? How did Peter know it was Elijah and Moses on the Mount of Transfiguration (Matt. 17:4)? What was Jesus writing in the sand (John 8:6, 8)? Did Adam and Eve have belly buttons? What was God doing before creation?

The sad thing is that many people divide over issues that are speculative and subjective. I don't want you to do that. I want you to be able to distinguish between these issues, preaching the fullness of the gospel and having grace in the things that should not divide.

Learn this phrase by seventeenth-century theologian Rupertus Meldenius: "In essentials, unity; in nonessentials, liberty; in all things, charity."

Why do we need to consider all of this? Because we are on a mission for our entire lives. We are called to "preach the word" (2 Tim. 4:2). We need to know what "the word"—the gospel—is in order to preach it.

The essence of the gospel is this: Christ, the eternal God-man, loves you and died for your sins, rose from the grave, and is king over the entire universe. We must call on him to have mercy on us and forgive us for our sins. If people truly do this, they are disciples of Christ. They are in God's family. If they do not trust Christ, they face the eternal judgment of God.

Your job in this mission is to contribute to the spreading of the glories of the gospel however you can. You are God's representative here on the earth. He has called you to "go therefore and make disciples." You may be called to be a foreign missionary (one who travels to countries where the gospel is not known), you may be called to serve on the audio-visual team at church, you may be called to sing in the worship band, you may be called to be a pastor, you may be called to be a godly mother, or you may be called to be a schoolteacher. Whatever your calling may be, you are to live a missional life.

Always be ready to give a reason for the hope that lies within you with gentleness and respect, because when you are living a life devoted to Christ (1 Pet. 3:15), people will want to know about the object of your faith. Are you living a life that shows your love for him? This life is a mere ant step. So tell this good news to everyone you can in every opportunity God gives you. And fear not, Christ's power is with you from beginning to end.

DISCUSSION QUESTIONS

1. Many people believe that faith is a very personal thing that is not meant to be shared with others. Explain why someone would say this. Explain why this belief is wrong.
2. What is the biggest fear you have in sharing your faith?
3. We discussed how Christ prefaced the Great Commission by saying that he had all authority. How does this comfort you in your mission?
4. Why do you think that Christ entrusted sinful people with spreading the gospel (instead of angels or himself)?
5. How have you seen nonessentials of the faith emphasized, instead of the main points of the gospel?
6. Explain the gospel in two sentences.

ADDITIONAL DISCIPLESHIP TRAINING

Evangelism and the Sovereignty of God, J. I. Packer

The Soul-Winner: or How to Lead Sinners to the Saviour, C. H. Spurgeon and Fleming H. Revell

Witnessing without Fear, Bill Bright and Billy Graham

Conclusion

I know you have many questions. I have been at this discipleship thing for decades now, and I *still* have many questions. But I am so pleased that you have made it through this book. Selfishly, I am even more pleased that I could be your guide. I pray that we have made strides in establishing a solid foundation for your faith. But remember, discipleship is a slow process. You have only begun. The ten chapters we have worked through are simply the beginning. They are an essential beginning, but there is so much more to learn. It is never-ending.

Augustine of Hippo gave us one of the earliest definitions of *theology* (the study of God): "faith seeking understanding." What he was trying to express is that first we become believers, and then we spend our entire lives seeking to understand our faith.

I teach theology for a living for a ministry I started called Credo House Ministries. You cannot comprehend how much I love my job. However, there is a downside to teaching faith and theology. Sometimes people become arrogant. Sometimes they become know-it-alls. Sometimes they look down on others who don't know or don't believe as much as they do. Yes, you may be passionate about truth (and I hope you are). Yes, you may know more than the average Joe (and I hope you do). And yes, someone is going to disagree with you about many things. But we must always have grace and patience with people. After all, remember how much time it took you to come around. People don't usually come around overnight, and if you have an arrogant, belligerent attitude, they, humanly speaking, might never come around.

My friend Dan Kimball wrote a book called *They Like Jesus but Not the Church*. The book expresses how some people really want to like Christ, but they hate Christians. It is easy to be unnecessarily offensive in our pride, clichés, and unthoughtful lives. The gospel is offensive enough without our attitudes adding to the offense. We are to be gracious, kind, understanding, empathetic, and forgiving. I expect this from you.

But I expect more from you. I expect you to carry on in your discipleship, following your Master, who never fit any mold. Do not be a conformer, but a reformer. Do justice. Love mercy. Keep the gospel pure. Never give up in pain. Show grace at every turn. Always tell of Christ through your words and deeds. Worship God in mystery and in truth. And keep studying God's Word.

I can't wait to meet you here or in eternity.

General Index

Scripture Index